Wife of...

To The "Wives of"

Doctors

Plumbers

Small-time
and
Big-time
Executives

Congressmen

Members of Parliament

Senators

Ministers

Mr. Secretaries

Any Powerful Jobs
and
Ambassadors

Wife of...

An Irreverent Account of Life in Powertown

Sondra Gotlieb

ACROPOLIS BOOKS LTD.

WASHINGTON, D.C.

ACROPOLIS BOOKS LTD.

Colortone Building, 2400 17th St., N.W.
Washington, D.C. 20009

Printed in the United States of America by

COLORTONE PRESS
Creative Graphics, Inc.
Washington, D.C. 20009

Attention: Schools and Corporations

ACROPOLIS books are available at quantity discounts with bulk purchase for educational, business, or sales promotional use. For information, please write to: SPECIAL SALES DEPARTMENT, ACROPOLIS BOOKS LTD., 2400 17th St., N.W., WASHINGTON, D.C. 20009.

**Are there Acropolis Books you want
but cannot find in your local stores?**

You can get any Acropolis book title in print. Simply send title and retail price, plus 50 cents per copy to cover mailing and handling costs for each book desired. District of Columbia residents add applicable sales tax. Enclose check or money order only, no cash please, to: ACROPOLIS BOOKS LTD., 2400 17th St., N.W., WASHINGTON, D.C. 20009.

Library of Congress Cataloging-in-Publication Data

Gotlieb, Sondra.
  "Wife of"...An Irreverent Account of Life in Powertown.
    1. United States—Politics and government—1981—Anecdotes, facetiae, satire, etc. 2 Ambassadors' wives—Canada—Anecdotes, facetiae, satire, etc. 3. Ambassadors' wives—United States—Anecdotes, facetiae, satire, etc. 4. Washington (D.C.)—Social life and customs—1951- —Anecdotes, facetiae, satire, etc. 5. Canadian wit and humor. 1. Title.
E876.G67 1985 973.927'0207 85-18717
ISBN 87491-797-2

Contents

Introduction 9

1. When I Rises Up I Gets Confused 13

"Wife of" and The President 14
I am Your Hostess. Who are You? 18
The Ambassador's Ball at Palm Beach .. 23
Popsie Tribble's Social Manifesto 27
Power Lunching with Melvin Thistle, Jr.
  of State 31
Sunday *trop de zèle* — A Local Disease .. 37
The Goose Girl Becomes a
  Temporary Princess 40
Close-To's, Use-to-be-Close-To's and
  Pretend Close-To's 43

2. Stamped with Purple Ink 47

Doing the Shuttle-Huddle 48
Chic and Non-Chic Countries 52
"Wife of" Hires a Chef 56
Baron Spitte's Pink-Theme
  Ladies' Lunch 60

"Wife of" Wanders through the
Pierre Hotel—Barefoot,
en negligee, at 4 a.m. 65
The Congressional Chili Cook-Off
and the Potato War 69
A Gentleman-in-Waiting, or
Dexter Tribble Becomes a
Powerful Job 72

3. Inspecting the USA ... 77

Having a Nervous Breakdown in
the USA 78
"Wife of" Meets the Most Interesting
People 82
Popsie Tribble and "Wife of" Attend a
Political Convention 85
Powerful Jobs Attend a Fashion Show .. 88
Houseguest Anxiety 92
Cold Pasta and Politics 96

4. Tribal Customs in the USA 101

Sonny Goldstone's Celebrity File 102
Carnal Passions in Powertown 106
Purposeful Fun in Powertown 110
The Space Shuttle Leaves "Wife of"
Behind 114
A-list and Election Parties 118
Popsie Tribble's White-Lie Technique . 121
"Wife of" Attends a Working Picnic 125

5. The Domestic Manners of the American 131

Thank-you Notes are a Way of Life 132
The Upper Media and Georgetown
    Chic 136
Gift Atrocities 139
The Washington Charity Ball 143
Powertown's Post-New Year's Blues ... 146
Inaugural Indignities—The Podiatrist
    and The President 149
Laughter Nights in Washington 152

6. Powertown Players ... 157

Popsie Tribble and the Balance
    of Terror 158
Joe Promisall, the World's Most
    Expensive Lobbyist 162
Social Triumphs of a Washington
    Hostess 166
Golden Hands and the Jell-o Collector . 170
The Quail Breast and Crayfish Circuit . 174
The Fast Lane 177

7. More Perils of Powertown 183

Mr. Rochester's Mad Wife and Embassy
Party Life 184
The Real Senator Pod 188
With Cooking Comes Power 192
Official and Non-official Dogs 197
The Lionel Portant Round Tables 203
Vacation Mistakes 206

Introduction

I think of "Wife of" as a humorous social commentary on the way temporary power and temporary status react upon human beings, including myself. The book is about the experience of being a wife of a foreign ambassador to the United States. Some of these experiences have appeared on the Op Ed page of *The Washington Post* in the form of a letter home to a fictional friend named Beverly.

I've been asked by readers about the identity of the characters in my letters. Are they fictitious or are they real? Who is Popsie Tribble, the Washington socialite? Who are Melvin Thistle, Jr., from State, and Lionel Portant, World Famous Columnist and Media Star? Who are Sonny Goldstone, the Gilded Bachelor and Social Asset, Senator Pod, Congressman Otterbach, Baron Spitte, the dusty diplomat, and Joe Promisall, the world's most expensive lobbyist? They are nobody and everybody.

Popsie Tribble is the devil in all of us, the Great Destabilizer who makes you feel inferior.

Lionel Portant represents the important Fourth Estate, so powerful in Washington; "power without responsibility" as a Mr. Secretary or White House Person might say. Melvin Thistle, Jr., from State naturally is a composite of high-rising and high-pressured officials, and Baron Spitte has the common sense and idle nature of the old-fashioned kind of ambassador. I think Spitte had a posting in London at the same time Prince Tallerand was there.

Sonny Goldstone is a Profitable Job, who is more at home in New York than Washington. Joe Promisall, the world's most expensive lobbyist, is Powertown incarnate.

Some people believe they know who Popsie and Lionel Portant actually are. They whisper names in my ear of people I've never met and sometimes never heard of. I consider this a compliment.

A short while after my letters began appearing in the *Post*, I attended a ladies' luncheon in my pseudo-official capacity as the wife of the Canadian Ambassador. (I say pseudo-official because I have no job description and I don't fit into any bureaucratic hierarchy. You might say that I'm the unpaid manager of a small hotel.) The woman on my left at the table said, "Aren't you the one who writes those letters to Beverly?" I admitted the fact. "Don't you think," she said, "that it's undignified for an ambassador's wife to make fun of herself and her husband in the newspaper? For a moment I was nonplussed, but encouraged by the sympathetic laughter from the others at the lunch, I said truthfully, "I was a writer long before I became a dignified ambassador's wife. Being a writer, I suppose, comes more naturally to me than being dignified."

She is the only person who has ever told me that I shouldn't make fun of myself given my exhalted position and temporary status. Most of the letters that I receive about my writing start off with this sort of sentence: "Until I read your letter to Beverly, I always thought ambassadors' wives were stuffy and unapproachable." In many people's minds, dignity connotes stuffiness, especially in connection with diplomatic life. Stuffiness is a characteristic I dislike in other people. Why is it necessary for me to be stuffy just because I became the wife of an ambassador for the first time in my life?

The two other most frequently asked questions concerning my writing are: "Does your husband approve?" and "How did you get started?"

My husband approves and acts as occasional censor. As long as he is ambassador to the United States and I am "wife of" we both believe my writing should be apolitical. I don't comment on the policies of Republicans or Democrats, or Liberals and Conservatives in Canada. He'd probably get fired if I began to preach on political issues. I tread a fine line. It's his job to see that I don't fall off and embarrass my countrymen.

When I lived in Ottawa, I did a lot of freelance journalism, and wrote four books, including two novels. I didn't worry about giving parties, managing a staff or meeting new people. During my first year and a half in Washington, my new role as wife of the ambassador left me too exhausted to do any writing except for the odd travel piece and a small op-ed piece about Canada, in *The New York Times*.

Meg Greenfield, the Editorial Page Editor of *The Washington Post*, saw it and asked me if I could do a piece for her some time. A year went by after her request before I wrote to Beverly. By that time, I figured that she'd given up on me. I simply hoped that I'd be able to write enough letters for a book, "Wife of". By sheer coincidence I bumped into Meg the day after I finished my first letter, and suddenly, with a good editor's instinct, she asked me again if I was doing any writing. I reluctantly showed her the letter, believing it too frivolous for her section. But she seemed to like it and asked me to do another. That's how the whole thing got started in the *Post*.

My first plan, to write about my experiences for a book, has now come to pass. It's supposed to make you laugh at "wife of" Mr. Ambassador, and the human failings of Powerful and Profitable Jobs (including Supremely Powerful and Profitable Jobs), Gentlemen-in-Waiting, Close-Tos and Used-to-be-Close Tos, and Popsie Tribble, who loves to get her picture in Woman's Wear Daily. If "Wife of" succeeds in making you laugh, I shall be satisfied.

1.
When I Rises Up
I Gets Confused

"Wife of" and The President

Dear Beverly,

You were right. There was something peculiar about my hair in that photo of me shaking hands with President Reagan. Actually, I wasn't supposed to be in that picture, because I'm only the wife of the Ambassador. In Washington, married women are known as wives of famous jobs or countries. Some of the wives have their own jobs, but that doesn't count except for Justice Sandra Day O'Connor. I was at a luncheon for 50 ladies where each one stood up and was introduced as the wife of the Nuclear Regulatory Agency, the wife of the Air Force, and I was presented as the wife of Canada, coming just after the wife of Peru.

The picture you saw in the newspaper was Allan presenting his credentials to the president. Before we met the president in his Oval Office they took us to another room, where some anxious young men told us where to stand, how long to speak and when to shove off. They told me that only Mr. Ambassador (that's what the Americans call my husband) was to have his photo opportunity with the president, in front of the fireplace. Wife of Mr. Ambassador was supposed to move away from the fireplace and out of camera range.

Well, you know how they used to describe me at home: "When she rises up she gets confused." After the handshake I backed into the camera crew. Some of the young men began to hiss at me, but the president grabbed my arm and insisted I be in the picture too. I really didn't want to have my picture taken with the president because I know my hair looked like corkscrews. But I didn't have enough time to tell the president about this hairdresser with the gold chains who had just given me the worst permanent in my whole life and that it was going to be weeks before I was photographable. Mr. Ambassador thought I should wear a snood if I went where people could see me. But I don't think they sell snoods in Washington.

Aside from meeting the president, the best thing about presenting credentials is being part of a motorcade. It was only a little motorcade with rather run-down D.C. police cars fore and aft. The man from protocol said that if we were delayed by traffic they would turn on the sirens and go through red lights. Mr. Ambassador said we had plenty of time and we oughtn't make a spectacle of ourselves. But the protocol man saw that I was disappointed and whispered something to the driver. We went through three red lights and the sirens were gratifying.

We presented credentials a few weeks after coming to Washington. I must say our departure was not auspicious. We left Ottawa very early in the morning. And you remember how late we went to bed the night before. I saw you putting away that cognac at the farewell dinner for us at the American Embassy, Beverly, so you know what I must have felt like when the landing gear in the plane refused to close on takeoff. It was frozen, so we had to return home and get into another plane. Ottawa was 40 below. It reminded me of our only other diplomatic arrival, 25 years ago when we were posted to Geneva. We took a lesser Cunard and a boat train, and then another train from Paris to Geneva. This wouldn't have been so bad except we were traveling with our children, 9 months, and 23 months, both in diapers, sea-sick and off their circadian rhythms.

They hadn't slept for 36 hours by the time we got on the overnight express to Geneva. I lay on one bunk with the girl, and Mr. Third Secretary lay on the other bunk, with the boy. They thrashed and drooled until 5 a.m. and then we all fell into a deep sleep. We woke awash in wet diapers, to the sound of the porter yelling "Genève, Genève." Mr. Third

Secretary stuck his unshaven head out of the window and stared at the senior officer (his boss), who was meeting us and who yelled, "You have two minutes to get off the train, unless you want to go to Bern." We passed sodden babies, seven suitcases, packages of paper diapers through the windows, threw our coats over our pajamas and followed the rest of the goods through the window.

Relative to this, our entrance to Washington was quite ambassadorial. This time Allan was senior officer, so the people from the embassy were more polite and numerous. Our chauffeur drove us to the Residence.

This word Residence is used instead of embassy or house to describe where the ambassador and "wife of" actually sleep. The Residence functions as something between a private home and a public drinking place. Although we are supposed to feel as if this is home, a lot of strangers come through the doors, so it's a little like living in a small hotel with the "wife of" as the manager. But I didn't know about that until later.

When I walked into the Residence a man dressed in black, who looked like Bluebeard's butler, handed me a set of keys and introduced me to maids, chefs and a few others. There was also a woman standing there who told me she was my social secretary. They were all waiting for me to say or do something. I asked the butler what one of the keys was for. "The downstairs storeroom," he said. "What's in it?" I asked. "Fifty cans of peas and two of tomato." I showed him another key. "That locks the thermostat so no one but madame can touch it." I've always wanted to be a boss, Beverly, but being the only one allowed to fool with a thermostat is not my idea of real power. So I told him I didn't want any keys and ordered a rye and soda.

I was feeling gloomy. Mr. Ambassador had left me to go to his office, the Chancery. It had been all of one day since he had been in his last. Thirty years of office-going does that to a person. So I was alone in this place, with the butler, maids, and chef. I'll tell you more about them later. Love. And take care of that hibiscus plant. I kept it going 10 years. It needs a bug blast every three weeks. The stronger the better. Actually the ones with health warnings on the can do the best job.

Your best friend,
Sondra

I am Your Hostess.
Who are You?

Dear Beverly,

I am sorry about your marriage. If it gives you satisfaction, change the lock on the wine cellar. Then he won't sneak back and steal the best bottles while you're at work. Concentrate on your new job because you might meet some famous people.

We didn't know anyone famous in Ottawa, except Margaret Trudeau. This has been a real handicap for me since we arrived in Washington. The problem is I have no other names to drop.

Everyone in Washington knows somebody famous. If they're Californians in the administration, they know Bob Hope and the queen. The lawyers, lobbyists and press start their conversations with "When I had dinner with Henry last week" or tell how George Shultz cooks steaks directly on the hot ashes of his fireplace.

Well there we were, Beverly, having to give our first party in Washington without knowing anyone famous. The only important people we knew when we arrived were the Tribbles. You remember them from the old days. Even then they had names to drop. Well now they live here and Popsie Tribble is a Washington socialite. "In Washington," Popsie said, "if you want people to come to your party, you have to make it in honor of somebody very well known." "You mean the president?" I asked. "Don't be stupid," she snapped. "He doesn't do embassy parties. But try the vice president." "Don't you think that would be pushy?" I said. "I don't know him." Popsie sighed. "Everyone knows the vice president except you. He's probably too busy anyhow. You have the wrong attitude. Remember you're asking people over for your country's sake. Don't look upon this as a personal thing."

You know how Popsie always had a good opinion of herself. So I wasn't surprised when she said: "Why don't you give a large party in honor of us? It will help Canada." But Mr. Ambassador didn't want to and said that we were going to give a party in honor of our foreign minister, who was coming to Washington on a private visit. An official visit, I learned later, is better because the famous and powerful have to come because of protocol.

I didn't have a clue whom to ask, but Mr. Ambassador and his staff suggested a list of names, which included the secretary of defense, the secretary of state, the ambassador to the U.N. and lots of stars from the press. Since I didn't know any of these people, I wasn't surprised when they didn't say yes or no when our social secretary rang them up. It was more worrying two weeks later when they still hadn't responded and the party was only six days away. We had the minister coming, and his Ottawa entourage, a protocol person from State and the Tribbles. Mr. Ambassador said if the worst came to worst, we could wire the minister to cancel and ask him to return when we knew some powerful people. But that would have meant loss of face, and ambassadors are supposed to avoid that. My social secretary explained to me that everyone put us on hold, an old Washington custom. If you put someone on hold you can wait and see if a better invitation comes in. As we mulled over the idea of cancelling, our social secretary called. "Two acceptances," she said gleefully. "Haig and Weinberger. Now everyone will come." They had accepted within five minutes of each other.

According to the newspapers, these two secretaries weren't talking to each other. Did one have an invitation mole in the other's office? Anyway, after they accepted, the phones didn't stop ringing — all acceptances. I wondered if our phone lines were tapped. Even Popsie Tribble knew about the acceptances and rushed over to tell me what to do. "Why don't you strew jasmine over the tables?" she said. And then she told me that she thought our place was kind of *petite bourgeoise* for a Residence. "You should try for a dream-like effect. And get rid of those embassy vases. They look like hospital catheters."

Well, Beverly, Washington is considered by some to be a southern town, but the florists here never heard of jasmine. "Are you sure it's a flower?" they asked. A knowledgeable fellow told me that a famous Washington hostess strewed her table with violets. He persuaded me that 50 bunches would make the Residence aristocratic enough for the Duchesse de Guermantes. Our butler, who was not one for the encouraging word, looked dubious when I brought them in the morning of the party. In the afternoon he was triumphant because they had shriveled into black spots and all you could see were green stems held by the rubber bands. "Shall I remove the violets, Madame, or do you still want to keep them on the tables?"

The only thing I remember about the food was that we couldn't cut through the *coulibiac*, because the crust was too tough. I had asked the chef to make a trial *coulibiac* for us the day before the party, but he didn't. Mr. Ambassador said I should have ticked the chef off instead of brooding about him in my bedroom. ("You must learn to assert your authority.")

The first snowstorm of the year occured on the night of our party. Mr. Ambassador was upstairs changing when most of the guests arrived 20 minutes early. In Washington during a little snow the people won't go out at all, or have Secret Service people or hired limousines bring them to the party well before the hour. I was idling by the front door, wondering if I ought to remove some artificial vines which had been decorating the toilet tanks in the downstairs bath-rooms since 1947. A man walked in and I said, "How do you do, I'm your hostess. Who are you?"

It was wrong, Beverly, what they reported in the papers back home. He didn't say, "I'm Caspar Weinberger, Mrs. Gotlieb, your guest of honor." He left out the guest of honor part, because he wasn't. The press garbles everything. Then about 20 strangers rushed in all at once and practically knocked us down. It still wasn't party time yet, Mr. Ambassador was upstairs, and I began to worry about crowd control. Popsie Tribble told me afterwards that I should have had a social secretary standing at the front door who would lead the guests to the drawing room where Mr. Ambassador and "wife of" stand by a crackling fire, underneath their portraits.

Anyhow, Mr. Ambassador finally descended, which was a good thing because he knew two more faces than I did. I kind of weaved in and out through the guests who appeared to know each other when I noticed a suspicous-looking fellow fooling around with an antique compact and box collection. As diplomatically as possible, I explained that these were not take-home souvenirs like Estee Lauder cosmetics, which are sometimes offered at balls and galas in Washington. He understood immediately and volunteered to introduce me to some of my guests. It turned out he was from the famous press rather than the working press (which means he eats at the Jockey Club instead of the Senate press lunchroom, which is not as nice as the Senate dining room). He trotted me through my Residence saying "Ambassador Kirkpatrick, meet the hostess," etc. Ambassador Kirkpatrick didn't say much to me except her comment about the dessert looking very Third World. I thought the statement pretty interesting and told Mr. Ambassador to put it in his telegram.

At 10:30 the whole crowd left, all at once, as if they were controlled by a secret signal from outer space, just like in Hitchcock's Birds. Popsie explained this was typical Washington behavior and no slight is meant to the hostess. "We get up early in the morning, dear, because we have to work so hard."

Beverly, I can't remember any conversation because I was too worried about people noticing the catheter vases and that there were no dinner plates on the table when the waiters brought out the lamb chops. Later lots of people sent hand-written thank-you notes saying they had a terrific time because they could feel the tensions between the secretary of defense and the secretary of state. Someone said they first heard that Gen. Haig was leaving his job, at our Embassy. No one told me a thing.

Beverly, don't come and visit me for a long time. Eighteen ministers are coming from Canada, a week apart, and they all want parties. I promise to look for an eligible famous male. But I need time.

Your best friend,

Sondra

The Ambassador's Ball at Palm Beach

Dear Beverly,

I think you and George are wise to go to a cheap Mexican fat-farm instead of Club Med. As you say, a diet of spring water and rice wafers for a week is bound to deepen the relationship.

I could do with a few days of zero calories myself because I just returned from an Ambassadors' Ball in Palm Beach. Beverly, we were never asked to balls in Ottawa. But here an Ambassadors' Ball is a kind of standard social event organized to raise money for the Descendants of the Veterans of the War of 1812 (our side won, Beverly) or whatever. I don't know why the presence of ambassadors and "wives of" is supposed to help fill the coffers. Certainly there is some controversy about how exciting they are. Popsie Tribble says an Ambassadors' Ball in Washington is one function she always avoids. When I asked her why, she said "There's something about ambassadors in large groups that puts me off. It's better to meet them on a one-on-one basis, preferably without the wife."

Popsie follows a social practice that is common in Washington. "When I give a party, the ratio between ambassadors and locals should be about 24 to 1." (The one includes "wife of.") "Otherwise things get very heavy, especially if Baron Spitte is there." The Baron, who is one of the last of the old-style dips, disagrees with Popsie about Ambassadors' Balls. Admittedly, Beverly, he is one of the dustier members of the corps, but his word carries some weight because he's been here almost as long as Ambassador Dobrynin. You have to watch the old Baron because he'll switch his place card at dinner if he thinks his *place à table* is lower than his rank. Popsie says the one good thing about him is that he has no wife.

The Baron told us it was our official duty to attend Ambassadors' Balls. A real aficionado, he never travels without white tie and decorations in case he stumbles on one in Muncie, Indiana, for example. We already had invitations to an Ambassadors' Ball in Dallas, Memphis and Palm Beach. The Baron encouraged us to go to Palm Beach. "They do very well by the corps: Moet and Chandon at breakfast and polo before lunch. The ladies wear some of the finest gemstones in the world. But you have to know how to foxtrot, my dear. It's very civilized and all for a good cause."

Unfortunately, we got off to a bad start. In mid-air, Mr. Ambassador realized he forgot his white tie and all the little buttons which he had bought especially for the Gridiron Club. (The Gridiron Club has nothing to do with football, Beverly. Once a year the Washington press invites famous politicians for dinner and insults them while they eat. The famous people are supposed to laugh and like the press better. More than that I don't know, because "wives of" are never invited. Ambassadors are considered neutral observers.)

When the plane landed a pleasant couple picked us up in their Rolls Royce and reassured us that Palm Beach was a community where most gentlemen have more than one white tie and set of little buttons. Mr. Ambassador would be looked after. They were our official hosts and their house, facing the ocean, was *"tout confort,"* as they say in the Michelin Guide.

"You have a free morning. Would you like to use our tennis courts or do some polo?"

I didn't tell them the last horse I ever saw was pulling a milk truck in Winnipeg 33 years ago. And Beverly, admit it, we did start off as tennis partners and then you dropped me for Gloria because you improved and I didn't.

Anyway, Mr. Ambassador only likes to do one thing. "I want to walk on the beach." Our hosts looked dubious. "We haven't been on the beach for years." I did notice that their skins were very white. "People who live in Palm Beach" they explained, "never go out in the sun. You can always tell a tourist by his tan."

But a wink is not as good as a nod to Mr. Ambassador. Early the next morning, he stole onto the beach and I had to follow him for several miles. Then we wandered about the house, which had an all-white motif, looking for our hosts, who had vanished. I wondered how we were going to spend the rest of our free morning when I noticed that the white marble floors were covered with black prints, as if two dirty dogs had just run amuck. Except that the prints were human and our feet were black with tar. My first instinct was to leave immediately for St. Petersburg but Mr. Ambassador wrapped his feet in his new dress shirt, made me wrap mine in his pajamas, and we spent our free morning on our knees, scrubbing the floors with Prell Shampoo and Kleenex. I wouldn't let Mr. Ambassador use the towels. "This never happens to Baron Spitte," I said bitterly. Luckily, Beverly, when our hosts appeared, all you could see were little bits of white lint from the Kleenex on the white marble floors. Our hosts looked puzzled but nobody said a word.

At the ball we queued up with the rest of the ambassadors (Baron Spitte was first), and shook hands with a thousand people. Every man in the place wore decorations except for you-know-who. The Baron's 24-year-old nephew, Prince Kiki, had to walk bent over because of the weight of his double row of medals. Some people wondered which war he had fought in. Mr. Ambassador, who is not as worldly as you might think, asked me why Kiki was foxtrotting cheek-to-cheek with his grandmother. The lady was wearing a diamond for every year of her life. But I knew they weren't related.

In the middle of the evening, Mr. Ambassador began to suffer from withdrawal symptoms because he hadn't read a newspaper since his arrival. He left the ballroom and sat in the hotel lobby trying to glean something from the "shiny sheets," the only reading material available. These are local magazines which show pictures of people having fun at balls.

Beverly, if they want you to foxtrot at the fat-farm, as an aerobic exercise, say no.

Your best friend,
Sondra

Popsie Tribble's Social Manifesto

Dear Beverly,

Popsie Trible dropped by looking marvelous in a suit designed for her by Oscar, and gave me a few tips about how I should behave. It was kind of her to take the time, since she has a pretty busy schedule being such a well-known socialite. She's always flying on private planes with exclusive names. I admit I do get tired of the names and planes. You wrote that I defer to her to the point of sycophancy, but, Beverly, I've seen you with her too.

Here's the gist of the conversation. "In Washington," she warned, lighting up a Balkan Sobranie, "parties aren't supposed to be fun for ambassadors' wives. Remember that you're sitting next to a job, not a person. Sondra, you have to charm the Powerful Job."

Well, I put my foot down a little bit. "Aside from the president, who do I have to be nice to?"

"Anyone who has a Job-That-Influences-Government-Policies." She ticked off the categories — "the Administration, Congress, the Lobbyists and the Press."

"What about rich people?"

"Powerful Jobs are more important than money in Washington, but money can't hurt."

Popsie's rich, so I think she was being straight with me. She was planning a party, and I asked her if she would seat me next to a Powerful Job who was warm and witty. But you know how tough she is, Beverly. Popsie said, "Any Powerful Job who is warm and witty sits beside me."

Popsie's right. Powerful Jobs come to parties to trade information with other Powerful Jobs they hadn't made contact with during the day. I don't have any information about the Middle East, the GNP or which Powerful Job is going to be fired. So I have to be the one to do the stroking.

"Should I be nicer to the men than the women?" I asked. "Well, I wouldn't snub Elizabeth Dole or Sandra Day O'Connor, or wives of Powerful Jobs, especially the second wives." "Second wives," Popsie repeated "have more influence because they are younger."

She was one up on me again. She's on her second husband and I'm still with Mr. Ambassador. I'm not sure if Popsie is younger than me but I let that one go.

Then she went on about social secretaries. "Embassy parties are usually the pits because of their bad advice. Usually they've been ensconced at the embassy since Pearl Harbor and give the new 'wife of' a rather nostalgic list of names. Remember, Sondra, in Washington everyone keeps their titles. Once a Mr. Secretary, always a Mr. Secretary. The same with Senators and Generals. Foreigners like you become confused." She went on. "I remember going to an embassy party where the 'wife of' a Mr. Ambassador thought she had invited a Mr. Secretary from the Reagan administration. In fact, he dated back to the New Deal."

Then Popsie startled me. "Beware of Embassy rats."

"We keep the Residence spotless," I said.

"Don't be silly. Those are the people who asked you to parties when you first came."

"What's the matter with them?" I asked.

"The only reason they're nice to you is that they want you to ask them back to the embassy. They won't mind if you only invite New Deal people with them. They just want to get dressed up and have a good time."

"Well, I like to do that too," I said.

Popsie shook her finger. "That's a fun party and you as the wife of Mr. Ambassador shouldn't waste your time with those." (There, Beverly, she goes too far.)

"What's worse than an embassy party?" I asked.

"Dinners at the Washington Hilton where two thousand people attend. It's like being at O'Hare Airport. There are always lines of people waiting to get through the metal detectors."

"You have to pass through metal detectors to go dinner-dancing at the Washington Hilton?"

"Of course. The only reason people go there is that the president or vice president is going to attend. Which means everybody has to go through security. It's at least a half-hour wait to get to your table. And the persons standing behind and in front of you are those you've been avoiding for the past 20 years."

"Isn't there a nice cozy place where people give parties in Washington?" I asked.

"Certainly," Popsie answered. "The F Street Club. Washingtonians love giving parties there because it's small, exclusive and looks like the shabby home of a well-born lady from Georgetown. Remember to pull down the blinds when you go upstairs to the bathroom. If you can find it. The window faces the chauffeurs waiting down below."

"Aside from the blinds, what's wrong with the F Street Club?" I asked.

"F Street Club parties are always black tie. So you get dressed up in your long dress and they push you out the door at 10 o'clock. I don't quite know why everyone goes home so early at F Street Club parties," Popsie admitted. "Maybe the old lady likes to go to bed early."

"But everyone in Washington likes to go to bed at 10:30," I interjected. "I remember being trampled down by a retreating crowd in our own hallway just when I started to have my first interesting conversation with a Powerful Job."

"What should I wear to black-tie parties, Popsie?"

"You're safest in a long dress with insignificant jewelry. It's only visitors from New York or Texas who actually wear necklaces. Political ladies in Washington would rather reveal their neckbones than their diamonds. It's because of the press. Never look too rich. Especially if there are photographers about."

"What should I avoid wearing?"

Popsie reflected. "No cleavages. On the other hand, avoid dresses with little bows tied at the top like you wore in Canada. An Ambassador's wife should be noticed. Wear National Dress."

"I have no National Dress."

"Then wear lots of sequins. Sequins attract Powerful Jobs."

There you have it, Beverly. Popsie's social manifesto. Glad to hear your muffin shop in the basement mall is beginning to make a profit.

Your best friend,
Sondra

Power Lunching with Melvin Thistle, Jr. of State.

Dear Beverly,

Well, our latest disaster happened when we invited Melvin Thistle, Jr., from the State Department to a fancy restaurant. You remember Baron Spitte, one of the dustier members of the dip corps? The Baron told Mr. Ambassador that Thistle Jr., was the man to cultivate, if he wanted a Powerful Job to pause and reflect upon the Good Neighbor to the North. "Don't hide him away at the embassy for lunch; it's very prestigious to be seen eating with Thistle in public."

There's another Washington rule, Beverly. Never go to a fancy restaurant with a nobody. I once took my Auntie Zora, who's hardly a nobody in Gravelbourg, Saskatchewan, and the headwaiter put us at a table closer to Gravelbourg than to where Lionel Portant, the World Famous Columnist and TV Commentator, was sitting.

At Washington restaurants, who you are designates where you sit. I would even say some of the shallower types care more about the seating than the eating.

Anyhow, Beverly, I spoke to "wife of" Thistle who never goes to embassy dinners ("too noisy"), but graciously decided to put up with our company when I invited her and Thistle to this place that's supposed to be the alpha and omega of gastronomic experience. "To tell you the truth, Sondra, we only eat out at Roy Rogers because of Melvin's salary." We met "wife of" at the restaurant. (Thistle was late as usual — I think Chad was heating up.) We went downstairs.

Beverly, there's another funny thing about Washington restaurants. A great many of them are in basements, although they don't charge basement prices.

This time we were placed at a table gratifyingly close to Lionel Portant, who was dining with a White House Person. When Thistle walked in there was a lot of standing up and handshaking, which is always done in Washington restaurants when Important Jobs sit at adjoining tables. Everyone was whispering about the collection of power in our part of the restaurant. It really was quite a heady experience for me, although Mr. Ambassador says I over-react to such things.

The first ominous thing that happened, Beverly, was that Thistle, who's not known as an abstainer, refused a drink. I didn't take this as a complete diplomatic snub because "wife of" came through and ordered Scotch Mist. You should try one, Beverly; quite delicious, sipping crushed ice and whiskey through a straw, like a frostee freeze for adults.

While "wife of" and I drained our glasses, Thistle and Mr. Ambassador kept jumping up to shake hands with men who had just finished shaking hands with Portant and the White House Person.

All this jumping while Powerful Jobs paraded by our table must have unhinged me because I jumped up and held out my hand to a man I thought was Baron Spitte, but who turned out to be the headwaiter. Beverly, I swear he was a dead ringer, but Mr. Ambassador says if that was so, why didn't "wife of" Thistle stick out her hand to be kissed too. After Mr. Ambassador pulled me back into my seat, things got worse. Spitte's double loomed over us and began a recitation. The recitation consisted of all the chef's special-ties that were better than those printed on the menu. Well, I was in such a panic that I couldn't concentrate and forgot everything he said except the first and last dishes, Hot Duck Livers with Apricots and something that sounded like

Frogs' Legs with White Chocolate. (You know these *nouvelle cuisine* combinations, Beverly.) I hoped someone at our table who wasn't intimidated would bring him to heel and ask for a repeat. But Thistle's attention had wandered and he was straining to hear what the White House Person was saying to Lionel Portant. Mr. Ambassador was cocking an ear in that direction too. I hadn't lost my head completely because I was the only one who noticed that Spitte's double didn't mention any prices during the speech.

But I hadn't the sangfroid to ask if the Duck was more expensive than the Frogs and besides I was the hostess. Confidentially, Mr. Ambassador was a bit shaken afterwards when he discovered an $80 difference between the two. I can't remember which took the jackpot.

Naturally, everyone ordered the first and last dishes (all we could remember), except Melvin Thistle, Jr., who, to my horror, asked for poached eggs.

Beverly, I'll say this for Washington headwaiters. They know their business, which is not food, but people.

If Thistle from State wanted poached eggs instead of duck livers that was perfectly all right. Not a sneer or even a disappointed comment. But I don't think Auntie Zora could have got away with it.

You see, Beverly, Spitte's double knew something about Washington that I didn't know. Anyone with power is on a diet. After Thistle Jr. ordered, "wife of" cleared her throat and said, "Melvin has to watch his weight."

Well it wasn't auspicious, Beverly. Have you ever tried to have an all-embracing geopolitical conversation with Melvin Thistle on Washington water (Perrier gives him gas) and poached eggs? I needn't have worried. Spitte's double called Thistle to the phone and he disappeared for the rest of the meal.

There was nothing left for the rest of us to do except continue eavesdropping on Lionel Portant and the White House Person, who, you've guessed it, Beverly, were eating poached eggs. I tried to chat with "wife of," but the name

Thistle kept coming up at the next table, so we were all riveted. Mr. Ambassador said he discovered what Thistle had proposed to the president during a National Security Council meeting.

Now Mr. Ambassador doesn't bother so much with Thistle, he learned his own Washington lesson. If you can't reach Melvin Thistle, Jr., take Lionel Portant out for dinner.

Be sure and remember me when you are planning your face lift, Beverly. Popsie Tribble says there's some interesting scientific data which prove that "wives of" get wrinkles at a younger age in Washington than in any other city.

Your best friend,
Sondra

Sunday
trop de zèle—
A Local Disease

Dear Beverly,

You know how old Baron Spitte, the dusty diplomat, occasionally shares the secrets of the trade with Mr. Ambassador and "wife of." One Monday he saw us looking particularly haggard and said knowingly, "You're suffering from a local disease, Sunday *trop de zèle*. If you want to avoid it, you must get out of Washington from Saturday night until Monday morning."

Pas trop de zèle, Beverly, is a diplomatic phrase thought up by a pal of Spitte's, Prince Talleyrand. (I think they were in London together.) Loosely translated, it means the eager beavers never catch the worm.

Well, whatever you might think about the Baron's fustian little ways, he does have his insights.

Sunday has become our day of dread and fatigue. The blight begins before we get up. Two humongous newspapers are delivered to our door (one comes all the way from New York), and it's an exhausting and dirty ordeal trying to get through them early Sunday morning. My hands and face are always smudged with newsprint.

You might wonder, Beverly, why we bother with them at all. Well, we paid for them, of course. But more than that, Sunday seems to be the day when the locals like to give intimate informal brunches, lunches and dinners, where all the people written about and all the people who write in the newspapers gather together. And guess what they want to talk about, Beverly: their articles or themselves.

But it's not only the print people. There are the talking-head shows to contend with on television. Always on Sunday, just before the little parties, three different shows.

Our energy has almost drained out by noon racing through the newsprint so we'll be ready to concentrate on the screen and watch Meet-the-Powerful-Jobs, Meet-the-Powerful-Press and Meet-the-Powerful-Jobs-Meeting-the-Powerful-Press. But it's difficult getting the gist of what Melvin Thistle, Jr. is saying to David Brinkley about Nicaragua when you have to watch a Mr. Secretary telling Lionel Portant about the deficit or missile deployment.

We're flicking and reading, Beverly, flicking and reading, just so we'll have something to talk about when we see the Mr. Secretary or Thistle Jr. at one of the little parties.

Then "wife of" has to wash the black smudges off her face and worry about what she's supposed to wear to an informal Sunday lunch in Washington. From what I've observed so far, there's a dangerous latitude between the two forbidden costumes, sequins and blue jeans. If I decide on that fussy little number you made me buy in Toronto, Beverly—too many ruffles—they'll all be wearing something subdued but expensive, like Yves St. Laurent trousers and blouses. So far, "wife of" has never worn the right outfit to the right party.

Anyway, things could be worse because "wife of" has discovered three conversational openings that usually get her through the cozy little gatherings.

1. If she finds herself next to Lionel Portant, World-Famous Columnist, "wife of" should say, "I agree with what you wrote about missile deployment in your article today." "Wife of" doesn't have to know anything about missile deployment, but she must know he's written about it on that particular Sunday.

2. If she finds herself standing next to Melvin Thistle, Jr. from State, who's just been on television defending his position on missile deployment, which Portant has attacked,

"wife of" should comment, "I agree with everything you said. And you looked so thin and relaxed."

Now Thistle Jr. will fill in the missile gap that "wife of" missed when Mr. Ambassador was flicking the channels back and forth.

3. If she finds herself next to a Mr. Secretary who's undergone a bazooka attack on television and been told to resign by the New York City paper (possibly over missile deployment, maybe the deficit—"wife of" gets it mixed up): "Mr. Ambassador agrees with your position. If only the media really understood the issues, firsthand, in-depth, like you do."

Of course, Beverly, it's best to whisper these things in the ears of Powerful Jobs, so you won't be overheard. But to tell you the truth, as Popsie Tribble says, in Washington contradictory statements by "wives of" are not considered significant.

Now you understand why Sundays have become our day of dread and exhaustion.

Baron Spitte says there are three ways to avoid such Sundays.

1. Buy a country place in Virginia, preferably with its own tennis court and stables.

2. Buy a video tape and watch six Bette Davis movies instead of Meet-the-Portant shows.

3. Spend overnight in Baltimore and see the Bromo Seltzer Tower.

Well, Beverly, we followed Baron Spitte's cheapest advice. We visited the Bromo Seltzer Tower four times. The Baron was right: nobody from Washington was there. But we do need a little company on Sunday. So meet us under the Bromo Seltzer clock in Baltimore. It's just a 20-minute drive from BWI Airport.

Your best friend,
Sondra

The Goose Girl Becomes a Temporary Princess

Dear Beverly,

I'm sorry that the taxi driver in Calgary insulted you when you told him that Ottawa was your home town. It's kind of a stigma living in a government town even for someone like you who's not exactly a decision-maker. My only consolation is that Americans living outside the capital feel that way about Washington. I suppose it's because both cities are filled with bureaucrats and politicians who like power more than profit and don't seem to worry about bottom lines and deficits. (Are they the same thing, Beverly?) And both cities go in for urban planning, except that Washington does monuments and Ottawa does green patches.

Well, Washington and Ottawa may be one-factory towns, Beverly, but speaking for me, the resemblance stops there.

You knew my routine in Ottawa. Seven cups of coffee in the morning and then I'd drag myself to the typewriter. I'd never have to say "no calls" because nobody used to call me, except Mr. Peshke, the chicken and azalea man who'd occasionally ring me to find out if I needed a capon or a plant. Also, who was there to say "no calls" to? Once a week a cleaning lady would pick up the dirty laundry in the front hall and head for the washing machine. If the phone rang, I could rely on her to say "Nobody no home" and hang up without taking a message.

We did go to a couple of parties in Ottawa but since sameness and plainness are the camouflage of the Ottawa wife, I never worried about clothes. Beverly, when you first came from that gaudy town of Edmonton, I thought you were overdressed (although I didn't tell you that at the time). I have a vague memory of you at a Government House Skating Party, in a fox-tail boa, being helped off the rink by the "wives of" in parkas. I always played it safe. My uniform was a Ports dress with a little bow tie in front. The more I wore it, the more people respected me.

It's not the same in Washington. The first time I ever saw a sequin was in this Roman capital. Sequins go with monuments and power.

Well now Goose Girl has become some sort of Temporary Princess. I have a social secretary who takes messages. Yes, Beverly, people actually call me.

Dr. Garbfut wants to invite Mr. Ambassador and "wife of" to a dinner in honor of the Global Institute. The Cirrhosis of the Liver Foundation wants the embassy to give a midnight buffet. And our Lady Butler, who replaced Bluebeard's butler, calls to ask whether we want white wine or red and to tell me that the tablecloths are shrinking.

The difficulty is, Beverly, no one has ever heard of the Garbfuts or the Global Institute, Mr. Ambassador hates midnight buffets, and I forgot to order the white wine when Lady Butler reminded me last week. Two hundred people are coming for cocktails tonight and white wine spritzers is the favorite Washington drink. I told you about the cases of bourbon in the cellar. Nobody will touch it.

Anyhow I try not to think about shrinking tablecloths and tell the new chef, a 20-year-old Parisian, what he is supposed to do with maple syrup. Lady Butler asks if it's all right to use the finger bowls for dessert at the dinner we are giving the following night, because we haven't got anything else to keep the floating island pudding from slopping over the plates.

You can be sure that I'm fully dressed and wearing high heels when I go downstairs in the morning because I'm afraid I'll bump into the guests Mr. Ambassador has asked to breakfast. Breakfast guests are always male, because breakfast meetings are considered serious business in Washington. Beverly, have you ever done a seating chart? In Ottawa my guests used to sit on the stairs and spill food over their clothes and I never had to worry about who sat on the highest step.

In Washington, I have to put guests at round tables so that no one feels below the salt. It takes me a morning to do a seating plan. Here are some of the rules:

1. Make sure a Powerful Job graces every table.

2. Never put more than two Powerful Jobs at one table.

3. Never put Powerful Job next to World Famous Columnist because the latter always writes something nasty about the former on the day of your party.

4. Never put Powerful Job next to woman or "wife of" who does not know he is powerful.

5. It's best to have a man sitting next to a woman, but there are never, under any circumstances, an equal number of men and women.

6. Remember that Melvin Thistle, Jr., from the State Department, always comes late.

7. Expect three congressmen to drop out at the last moment and Popsie Tribble to call to ask not to put her next to Baron Spitte.

By the way, I'm thinking of buying a foxtail boa. Would you mind calling a few stores in Ottawa for me to find out the price? I'm sure they're cheaper at home. Unless you want to give me yours.

Your best friend,
Sondra

Close-To's,
Used-to-be-Close-To's
and Pretend Close-To's

Dear Beverly,

Popsie Tribble called me up the other day and asked Mr. Ambassador and me to a small dinner. "Nothing fussy," she said. That's Popsie's code for don't overdress, because the guest of honor is not in Dexter Tribble's income bracket and "wife of's" guest of honor might wear a tacky dress.

"The guest of honor," she continued, "works in a Think Tank." It's irrational, Beverly, but when I hear that phrase I see venerable, bearded men seated in a large metal receptacle, on top of a pole well above the populace, doing the world's worrying.

Anyway, to get to the point. Why was Popsie Tribble giving a party in honor of a Think-Tank Worker? Popsie only gives parties for famous names. "I never heard you mention him before," I said. "Has he just come to Washington?"

"Actually," Popsie replied, a little quickly, "he's been here for 20 years, but he's important because he's 'Close-To'."

"Close to what?"

"Close-to-the-Candidate."

Well, Beverly, I know you don't have much time to read the papers, but at least George must be aware this is election year in the U.S. as well as at home. Popsie went on.

"Although 'Close-To's' belong to both parties, they have several common characteristics. They don't have to be Powerful or Profitable Jobs, and their names aren't featured in Lionel Portant's columns. A 'Close-To,' " she admitted, "might even be owner of a muffin shop, like George. Of course the exception proves the rule. Dexter and I are acquainted with 'Close-To's in both parties who are famous movie stars. In any case, 'Close-To's are the only people the Candidate really trusts. 'Close-To's' may not want Powerful or Profitable Jobs for themselves, but they have the power to whisper in the ear of the Candidate on behalf of others."

Popsie lit one of her Balkan Sobranies and continued. "Naturally my Dexter knows all the candidates and is close to a present 'Close-To' in this administration." "But," she said, "the family of the Think-Tank Worker and that of the Candidate have shared a beach house in Rehoboth for 15 years. That's very close."

We came early to Popsie's party so she could further enlighten Mr. Ambassador and me about 'Close-To's.' Popsie was happy to teach us.

"You have to be careful during the election year. Be nicer to everyone. There are secret "Close-To's everywhere who might take offense if you're not aware of their connection."

That must be a hard act for Popsie, Beverly, because she believes in going to the top. Popsie doesn't bother with too many no-name Think Tankers. But election year makes Gentlemen-in-Waiting and Powerful Jobs (like her Dexter, who's been both) extra careful. "The problem," Popsie admitted, "is that it's hard to tell the difference between a real 'Close-To,' a 'Used-to-be-Close-To' and a 'Pretend-Close-To'."

"A real 'Close-To'," she continued, "never has political ambitions which might cause the Candidate distress. Some 'Used-to-be-Close-To's' have had their names cited once or twice in the those small, unprofitable, monthly magazines. Even this negligible publicity makes some of them uppity and less attractive to the Candidate. I was stung myself by a 'Used-to-be-Close To.' I had a luncheon for his "wife of" at the Jockey Club, not realizing that his phone calls were no longer being answered by the Candidate."

Popsie sounded rueful, and lit another Balkan Sobranie to erase the memory.

" 'Pretend-Close-To's' are easier to distinguish. Let's say that you encounter a 'Pretend-Close-To.' Being the wife of a Foreign Ambassador, you'll say something ignorant like admitting you never met or even heard of the Candidate. Beware, Sondra, if the 'Pretend-Close-To' suspiciously over-responds by saying he was with the Candidate in high school, the Army, the movies or Divinity School and then promises to introduce you to him tomorrow. There will never be a tomorrow. The 'Pretend-Close-To' is a Lobbyist merely working the room. The Candidate, as everyone knows (except you), is already in Tampa preparing for a speech."

Popsie finished her lecture moments before the guests arrived. As the doorbell rang, she leaned over us and whispered.

"Remember, my 'Close-To' is a listener, not a talker. He won't offer you any introduction to the Candidate and will only mention his name late in the evening."

Beverly, it was my turn to sit next to the Think-Tank Worker during coffee. I said, "The election campaign must be tiring for the candidates."

"Indeed," Close-To the Candidate replied, mentioning him by his first name. "-------called me yesterday to say he intended to rest at our beach house in Rehoboth for a couple of days. I sent my wife there to clean the place up. That's why she's not at the Tribbles tonight."

Popsie's one step ahead of everyone in Powertown. Beverly, she's the first hostess this year to have a made a "Real Close-To" a guest of honor.

Your best friend,
Sondra

2.
Stamped with Purple Ink

Doing the Shuttle-Huddle...

Dear Beverly,

I'm glad you're coming to Washington at last although I'm not sure what you mean by "doing some market research on muffin shops." If you're looking for a profitable site, Mr. Ambassador thinks Georgetown has the greatest number of the classic muffin-eater type.

But I'm worried about you flying in on the shuttle from New York. Taking the shuttle for the first time at your age is like learning to ski without an instructor. The shuttle has a set of rules particular to itself which covers everything from social behavior to arrival expectations.

Beverly, you really ought to have an old shuttle salt put you through the paces because it will be shocking experience. I know you think Washington is a glamorous town but even Popsie Tribble, on her way to a gala benefit in New York, looks like a deportee when she's on the shuttle.

So if you actually make it from New York, don't expect me to introduce you to any Important Job hanging around the airport. You won't be in bandbox condition. Oddly enough, Popsie Tribble actually believes the shuttle encourages spontaneous travel because you don't need reservations and it is supposed to leave every hour. She says, "When I get pooped out shopping at Bergdorfs I grab a cab to La Guardia and soon I'm flying back to Georgetown in time for Baron Spitte's costume ball."

Well, Beverly, Mr. Ambassador and "wife of" have never been that lucky. Here's our shuttle drill from Washington's

National (a must, Beverly, because of your interest in architecture; Early Greyhound, I'd say).

We try to arrive with a positive attitude because they said on the phone that the weather was hunky-dory and planes were leaving on time. But Mr. Ambassador, who has a bionic nose, sniffs fog over the East River in New York. And the terminal is ominously empty as we make our way to Shuttle Gate 18.

Beverly, at Gate 18, we meet with Shuttle Reality.

An assemblage of bodies looking like the cast from Mother Courage, with 50-pound bundles strapped to their backs, are doing the Shuttle Huddle. They do the Shuttle Huddle because there is no seat selection. Those who stand clamped nearest to the door where they think the plane is supposed to park will get the best places. Since no plane has left for New York since 6 a.m. (fog over East River) about 500 refugees are ready to risk suffocation in order to avoid the dreaded middle seat.

On normal plane trips, Beverly, the rules of social behavior are cut and dried. Don't make eye contact, keep your skirts drawn in, and place your carry-on luggage on the seat beside you so a stranger won't sit down.

These rules are more embarrassing to follow on the shuttle, even though we all make the attempt.

You see, Beverly, except for the odd tourist like you, everyone on the shuttle knows each other.

There's Lionel Portant, World Famous Columnist and TV Commentator, who broke bread at our residence two days before, with his head buried in *The New York Times* avoiding eye contact with Mr. Ambassador. Melvin Thistle Jr. from State is pretending to sleep standing up, because Joe Promisall, the famous lobbyist, talking anxiously on the pay phone, might hang up and talk to him. Joe Promisall used to have Thistle's job in a past administration, and, who knows, might get it again in the next.

Beverly, Powerful Jobs become Profitable Jobs when Powerful Jobs leave government. Profitable Jobs are more sociable unless they suffer from "decompression," a Washington code word for an emotional state caused by loss of power.

In the bleakness of Shuttle Gate 18, decompressing former Mr. Secretaries who used to fly on government planes to New York now have to press their bodies against people whose phone calls they never returned.

Some Profitable Jobs, like Joe Promisall, don't practice normal airplane rules. Joe behaves as if Gate 18 is one more Washington cocktail party. Wordlessly, he pats a former Four Star General on the back, slides over to Mr. Ambassador for a handshake and explains how he used to run the shop to Melvin Thistle, Jr., who is forced to open his eyes. Lionel Portant, with his instant TV recognizability, is now standing facing the wall praying nobody can see him.

Beverly, we have now been standing at Gate 18 for two hours and Mr. Ambassador is angry because I packed four pair of shoes and the electric hair curlers in one of the carry-on bundles. But it's a good thing I did, because Mr. Ambassador uses it as kind of a counter-missile to advance our boarding position and we are able to requisition an aisle and window seat.

Beverly, always glance at the bulkhead seats, because the shuttle, despite the no-reservation rule, will keep the bulkhead for famous people. Some of the Famous suffer from reverse snobbery and believe it's politically safer to sit discreetly several seats behind. No reverse snob, the dusty diplomat, Baron Spitte, is already ensconced in the bulkhead as we walk by.

The problem now is what to do with the bundles. Storage space is not a Shuttle Priority. Mr. Ambassador parks the counter-missile on top of Baron Spitte's cashmere coat in the overhead space for the Famous. I crawl on the floor and wedge my bundle in front of the dreaded middle seat (no space in front of mine) which has been taken over by unhappy Melvin Thistle.

It's another half-hour sitting on the runway and the atmosphere is deadly. Everybody except us foreigners is afraid to talk because an enemy is bound to be within hearing range. I don't dare ask Thistle why he's going to New York because if he answers he might reveal his foreign policy intentions to Joe Promisall, who's breathing heavily behind us.

Finally, we hear our pilot.

"Morning folks. I'm Charlie Williams. Just relax and have a nice chat with your neighbor. We're number 14 on the runway."

Twenty minutes later, Thistle speaks to me.

"If you trade seats with me, you will be closer to your luggage."

Before I answer, Charlie makes a second announcement. "Good news, folks. We have clearance from the tower. And I'm thrilled to say we have a truly famous person on our airplane."

Lionel Portant, all the ex-Mr. Secretaries, and even Thistle, try to remove a smug look from their faces.

"Let's welcome to our shuttle this morning the famous dog trainer and author of "No Bad Dogs', Barbara Woodhouse." Then he pauses and says, "We're ready for takeoff. Stewardesses, here is your command. Sit."

Beverly, I hope your trip to Washington is tax-deductible.

Your best friend,
Sondra

Chic and
Non-Chic Countries

Dear Beverly,

Popsie Tribble, the Washington socialite, came over
this afternoon and brought me bad news about my country.

"You have a heavy burden in this city, Sondra," Popsie
said. "Canada is just not chic."

I said naively, "I didn't know there were chic and non-
chic countries."

Popsie shook her head. "You could have guessed.
Socialites like myself don't fly up to Ottawa or Winnipeg to
parties."

She was right. Beverly, you know, I lived all my life in
Ottawa and Winnipeg and never encountered a socialite,
although I had met some socialists.

Popsie twisted the knife one more turn.

"Your whole country is simply not in. Do you read W?"

I didn't know what W was.

Popsie explained painfully. "It's a colour newspaper
written for the elite woman. It has many pictures of
socialites like me in designer dresses. Woman's Wear Daily
own it. An ambassador's wife from a chic country like
Britain or France knows she has the option of publicizing
her parties in W. You don't even have that option."

Popsie opened up a copy and pointed to an article
announcing who's in and what's out.

Beverly, Canada was in the out column along with the
Stuttgart Ballet and the Russian government.

"We would really like to be 'in'," I said. "How can we
become a chic country?"

"There are status symbols in Washington," she advised. "The best status symbol for an embassy is to have your own tennis court. The British and Swedish have their own courts. Anybody who's anyone wants to play tennis on a private embassy court. But," Popsie warned, "don't build a swimming pool. Swimming pools are middle-class and therefore 'out'. I have some friends who unfortunately built their swimming pools before they were 'out'. Now they put water lilies and sculptings in them to prove they are ponds and part of the landscape."

Beverly, what could I say? Popsie was right again. We have a wonderful middle-class swimming pool in our Washington residence and nobody has asked to use it. But we had been asked many times if we had a tennis court. There was no point putting in a tennis court. Aside from the uproar over the expense back home, we don't know how to play.

Then she asked, "Why don't you have a title? The British, the Australians and even the New Zealanders all have Lady and Sir in front of their names. A lot of Europeans are Countesses."

"We banished titles in 1935," I said bravely.

"A mistake. Americans love titles."

Then Popsie spoke more kindly. "You really ought to do something about those peculiar articles about Canada in *The New York Times*."

Beverly, you know what she is talking about. One appeared the other day about polar bears eating up the garbage dump in Churchill, Manitoba, my home and native province. Another announced in the inside pages that Nova Scotia, the seat of Confederation, was on the brink of secession. I telephoned Nova Scotia and was relieved to find out that they were as surprised as I was.

I explained to Popsie that Canada doesn't make the front page of the *Times* too easily. There was a time when we only received two notices in a decade. The National Gallery of Canada had brought a famous American collection to

Ottawa and *The New York Times* sent a critic who said the pictures were fake. The second time occurred when General De Gaulle stood on a platform in Quèbec (which was and still is part of Canada) declaiming, *"Vive le Quèbec libre".*

"Do we need another De Gaulle?" I asked.

"No," she admitted. "The problem is that you are just like our country cousins. It would be more chic if you spoke a foreign language."

I said, a little rashly, "We do, we do, we're bilingual, we speak French."

"Well," Popsie answered, "I'd cut out English entirely. It would make you more foreign and chic, like white truffles and *crème fraiche."*

To tell the truth, Beverly, Canada is not known for exotic foods in Washington. I just saw a supermarket ad for Ontario rutabagas, ten cents a pound. We really should charge higher prices. And there was some golden caviar advertised in one of those expensive food catalogues that arrive around Christmas. It was $40.00 for four ounces. I know we had the same stuff for $2.50 Canadian and very good it is. It comes from Manitoba where the polar bears eat our garbage and probably the caviar.

Beverly, why do we bore the media? Why do the eyes of journalists, anchormen, editors, publishers take on a glaze as thick as Quebec maple syrup when the word Canada is mentioned?

Popsie read my thoughts and asked, "Have you heard of a writer named Calvin Trillin? He writes for *The New Yorker,* which is chic. He says that Canada is 'out' too." I knew what she meant. Trillin had written a novel in which the villain, a muckraker for *Time-Week,* gets his come-uppance by being exiled as bureau chief in Ottawa. I remember how Trillin put it. "Cold Ottawa, boring Ottawa. Never in the Magazine Ottawa. Perfect place for King of the Schmucks Ottawa."

I was pretty depressed Beverly and Popsie didn't make things better when she told me my name was "out."

"Personally," she said, "I think Sondra is cute. But you should understand that we socialites all have names ending in ey, y or ie. There's Muffy, Buffy, Bitsey, Bootsie, Oatsie, Lucky, Vangie as well as Midge and Muffet. You should change your name. It's the least you could do for Canada."

Your best friend,
Sondra

"Wife of" Hires a Chef

Dear Beverly,

As you know, Popsie Tribble drops in every six weeks or so to tell me how to conduct my life in Washington. During one of her first drop-ins, she gave me three rules about managing the Residence.

"You must have a chef who can cook some edible national dishes.

"The butler should know your guests by name.

And, above all, Sondra, no pregnant maids."

Beverly, as I said, it was early days. The maid was pregnant. My chef was Turkish and specialized in that famous Canadian dish, shish kebab. And I'm afraid that our mournful butler announced Popsie as Mrs. Roosevelt.

"Is he thinking of Eleanor or Alice Longworth?" Popsie asked. "They'd both be near a hundred if they were alive today."

Popsie glanced anxiously at the mirror.

I tried to soothe her.

"Maybe he's thinking of Lucky Roosevelt, the Chief of Protocol" I said hopefully. "She's about our age."

Gracefully, Popsie accepted my theory. She knew I hadn't got a grip on things yet because there had been a to-do with the chef. I had insisted on fresh shrimp.

"No fresh shrimp in Washington, Madame."

"Nonsense," I said firmly. "Baron Spitte told me they sell fresh shrimp down by the wharf."

"No fresh shrimp down by the wharf, Madame."

Well, you know that Mr. Ambassador told me to assert my authority with the staff. I made the chauffeur drive me and the silent Mustapha to the wharf, where we saw fresh shrimp piled high in front of the vendors. Beverly, there were even little fishing boats behind the stalls, right on the water. I was triumphant. Mustapha and I went over to a stall. He poked a few fish uninterestedly while I spoke.

"Give me three pounds of fresh shrimp."

"Lady, we don't have fresh shrimp."

"What's that in front of me?"

"Defrosted shrimp. They freeze them on the boats in Carolina."

Mustapha spoke only once on our way home.

"No fresh shrimp in Washington, Madame."

The next time Popsie dropped in, I told her that Mustapha had quit.

"That's the way of all chefs," she said comfortingly. "They have a nomadic streak. Who's in the kitchen now?"

"A Bulgarian who's worked in 30 hotels, from Marrakesh to Salt Lake City. He's had lots of experience."

"Too much," Popsie decided. "There must be something wrong with him. Let's go in the kitchen and have a look."

It was 3 o'clock in the afternoon and the Bulgarian had a tumbler of whiskey in one hand while he basted some ducks with the other.

"He's drunk," Popsie said loudly. "I think you should fire him."

"Don't you think I should wait till after dinner?" I whispered. "There are 30 people coming this evening."

"Maybe that's wise," she agreed, and we went upstairs.

About half an hour later, the butler, with his little nervous smile, reported that the Bulgarian had walked out after throwing some of the ducks at the pregnant maid. Beverly, I knew it was Popsie's fault. He must have overheard her.

"Maybe I should call some of the other 'wives of' ambassadors and ask them how they find chefs."

"Don't be silly," Popsie said. "They'll think you're trying to steal the ones they already have. This is a cut-throat business."

"What am I supposed to do about tonight?"

Popsie realized I was panicking.

"Why don't you wipe off the ducks and I'll send in my person to finish off the cooking. Remember, this is the only time you can use her. She will only go to certain people in Washington. And she's always fully booked, but not tonight."

The lady came within an hour. She refused to give me her name.

"I do this evening because Mrs. Tribble asks me."

She told me that there would be strubbles for dessert, which worried me, but they turned out to be strawberries.

The next morning, I was still without a chef and Mr. Ambassador told me to put an ad in the paper.

We did get a lot of replies, Beverly, but they all swung in and out the kitchen door. The first chap, a Dane, was promising because he made a delicious fish and salad.

I told him to make something different the next day.

"I only do fish and salads. No meat, no desserts."

Beverly, eight chefs tried out, and none of them could put a meal together. It's because of hotel assembly lines where all these fellows had worked. The steak man never sees a fish, the pastry chef doesn't go near turkey, and the fish person can't make apple pie.

Well, it was panic-stations for me again when Mr. Ambassador said we had to give a dinner for our Prime Minister on short notice.

Popsie, of course, knew about his vital visit before I did.

"Am I on the invitation list?" she inquired.

I hedged. "The Prime Minister didn't really ask for you, Popsie. If a Powerful Job drops out at the last minute, I'll see what I can do."

"If I steal Baron Spitte's chef for you, will you put me on the list?"

For once, I knew what it was to wield power in Washington.

Popsie threw another chip on the table.

"Baron Spitte's chef can make Canadian national dishes. He used to own a restaurant in Montreal."

"You're invited."

Well, Beverly, Popsie and I sat down and planned the dinner.

"You'll have to hire a calligrapher to write the menus and place cards," Popsie said. "I know a nun who makes menu cards look like manuscript illustrations. And you should serve three wines, one Canadian, one American and one French — Chateau Petrus '75. Followed by vintage champagne, of course."

I was really excited when Baron Spitte's chef told me he was going to serve Canadian beaver tail soup. Melvin Thistle, Jr. of the State Department and World-Famous Columnist Lionel Portant were going to be impressed.

Beverly, the party was six weeks ago and it's taken me all this time to get over my depression.

Not one Powerful Job noticed the manuscript illuminations, and they thought the beaver-tail soup was consommé with a little gristle in it. They left the glasses brimming with Chateau Petrus. No one knew the mousse was made with maple syrup, and Baron Spitte didn't recognize his own chef's cooking.

I was furious with Popsie. "What's the point of worrying about chefs, calligraphers, vintage wines and national dishes?" I asked her. She told me that's the Washington paradox. People in Powertown don't really care what they eat or drink. But they know it if the fare is not as impressive as their power.

Baron Spitte has been to the Residence three times and still doesn't know I stole his chef. Don't tell him when you come.

Your best friend,
Sondra

Baron Spitte's Pink-Theme Ladies' Lunch

Dear Beverly,

Who was it who said the worst thing that can happen to a person is to have his fondest wish come true? Baron Spitte, the dusty diplomat who presented his credentials to President Nixon and whose chef I stole, has always ached for some Serious Media attention. Despite his passion for protocol, the Baron knows that conducting diplomacy in secret is no way to get your country onto the media's perforated map.

Beverly, there are more than 150 embassies in Powertown, and if the Media don't know you exist, the Powerful Jobs won't know either.

Well, yesterday, the Baron got what he always wanted, a full two minutes on the World News at 7, squeezed between the man-on-the-street interviews and the movie stars, and his name prominently mentioned in a column by World-Famous Journalist Lionel Portant.

Now he's marinating in his own bile and has fired his nephew and social secretary, Prince Kiki, who was only trying to help.

Until *l'Affaire Pink Ladies*, the old Ambassador lived a quiet life. The Baron could always be relied upon to be part of the ceremonies at azalea festivals, celebrity cook-offs and charity galas. The highlight of his year was the Ambassadors' Red Cross Ball in Palm Beach. The waltzing diplomat never missed a winter in 14 years, with Kiki always in tow, escorting the merry widows. They did get their picture in W and the shiny sheets, the Ambassador in white tie, head held high, and Kiki, a little bent over from the medals. But the Lionel Portant types considered the Baron and his hard-currency country too insignificant for their columns.

Not that he and Kiki didn't make an effort when they invited the Serious Media to the *Musicale.* But Popsie Tribble claimed it only made things worse. I was there, Beverly, and she was right.

The Baron, who is culturally minded (not an asset with the Powerful Press), takes singing lessons and entertained his guests before dinner with French Art Songs. My heart failed me when I saw all those little gold chains arranged in rows in the Tapestry Room. Prince Kiki was sitting upon a dais, waiting to accompany the Baron. Popsie, who knew what was coming, passed around NoDoz pills (that's what truckers take to stay awake on the road) which Lionel Portant churlishly refused. Since the Baron is confident enough to sing Wolf leider encores without the encourage-ment of applause, dinner wasn't served until 10 p.m. Naturally, the Serious Media, including Portant and a famous anchorman, fled without eating.

The total news blackout on the Baron and his country continued. He had tried tennis before the singing lessons. Beverly, Powerful Jobs will be nice to any ambassador with a respectable backhand, as long as he has a private tennis court. Well, the Baron's game was as bad as his singing, and there's only an algae fishpond at the back of the Residence.

It was Kiki who went to Joe Promisall, Washington's most expensive lobbyist, for help. Approachable Joe stood with his back to the 18th century log-burning fireplace in his office and said:

"Three things attract Powerful Jobs to Embassies. Tennis, Royalty and Charity. If you can combine all three, the media will have to put you on their map. The Baron's title is a plus, although it's too bad you can't get your country to fund a tennis court. I give this free advice to every new ambassador. In Washington, a tennis court is more important than an embassy dining room."

Joe Promisall isn't Powertown's most expensive lobbyist for nothing. He knows who's important, everywhere, even in Baron Spitte's insignificant little country.

"Don't you have a tennis-crazy Dowager Princess who can jump over a net at the age 80? I've seen a picture of that somewhere. Bring her to Washington and give a 'wives of' lunch in honor of her favorite charity. Which should have something to do with tennis if you want a bang-up crowd.

"If you can't get to know a Powerful Job," Promisall continued, "the next best thing is a contact with the wife. Her availability quotient is higher. If you get the wives out for lunch, the men will come for dinner."

Kiki had a good idea. The Baron would give a large ladies' lunch for the Princess' favorite charity—a retirement home for old athletes. And the ladies, except for wives of Powerful Jobs, who are always made honorary patrons (honorary patrons don't pay, Beverly), were asked to contribute $300 a head. That's a lot of money for lunch in the Baron's Tapestry Room, even in this charitable town. So Kiki added something else to pique the ladies' interest. All of us had to wear pink, the Princess' favorite color. And that's how Kiki's Pink Theme lunch began.

Beverly, the theme approach is not unusual in Washington. I've been to a bring-an-iris-lunch, a mad-hatter lunch, and even a "pretend we're in Hollywood lunch" where the place cards were a picture of a "wife of" and the movie star she was supposed to most resemble. You know that Popsie is always one-upping me, so I was kind of pleased when I got Grace Kelly and she was matched with Ethel Merman.

Kiki had a fantastic turnout. Almost 500 "wives of" Senators, Supreme Court Justices, Mr. Secretaries and Powerful Press showed up, obediently wearing a pink something as the blush-colored invitation requested.

Approachable Joe knew what he was talking about. Royalty, Charity and Tennis is the magic formula, and not only for Washington. Beverly, a flock of the Baron's merry widows, former "wives of" oil and real estate flew in from Palm Beach and Dallas. Waltzing diplomacy still has its uses, I guess. There were pink hats, and one lady from Palm Beach wore pink crocodile shoes. "Wife of" Portant was a little austere in a pink tennis warm-up suit. But then Popsie says she only shops at Tennis Lady. What surprised us is that she actually paid for her lunch. I wore that pink dress covered with the droopy petals; the one you says makes me look fat. Popsie was the most subtle. She wore her pink diamonds, which she had taken out from the vault for the first time in two years. But I think she was disappointed when she curtsied to the Princess and noticed the Dowager was resolute in black.

Joe Promisall had wangled it so there was a list of all our names and there were photographs in the paper, which in retrospect was a mistake.

Two months have passed, Beverly, and all the pink ladies are angry. It seems that Kiki personally supervised the collection of the lunch money, then disappeared without giving it to his aunt. Baron Spitte is especially angry. He got all this publicity. It was terrible, and now he has to pay Promisall for it anyway.

Phrases like "absconding with the funds" have appeared in Portant's column. Mr. Ambassador says Portant's too personally involved to write about Baron Spitte objectively. Unfortunately, the Baron hasn't a good TV image, and didn't appear sincere when he told the famous anchorman that Prince Kiki was still looking for old athletes, preferably tennis pros, in the mountain regions of his country.

But Beverly, don't you think he overreacted when he fired Kiki? After all, the Baron's face will be more familiar when he crowns the Queen of the Rhododendrons in Savannah next week.

Popsie's really mad because she had to pay for her lunch. But I'm not all that fussed. Kiki slipped up somewhere and made me an honorary patron.

Your best friend,
Sondra

"Wife of" Wanders through the Pierre Hotel Barefoot, *en negligee*, at 4 a.m.

Dear Beverly,

I swear I'm not going to stay in a hotel with Mr. Ambassador anymore. As you know, he has to travel because he's supposed to be Ambassador to the United States, not only Washington. But truthfully, sometimes Official Trips can be a trial. The straw that broke the back of "wife of" was when she was forced to wander about the Pierre Hotel in New York, barefoot, *en negligee* at 4 o'clock in the morning.

To be perfectly fair, I don't think it would have happened if Mr. Ambassador had been the first instead of the 14th speaker on the agenda at a black-tie dinner at another hotel across the street, the Plaza. Popsie Tribble says that sometimes "the right people" have tea in the Plaza lobby; but I wouldn't know because when I go to the Plaza it's to the ballroom for banquets and speeches. Anyway, according to Popsie, the tearoom is not all that exclusive. That's what she said when she heard you and George didn't have any trouble getting in.

The people who chose to listen to the speeches in the Plaza ballroom were Profitable Jobs and "wives of" from New York, bankers, brokers and men called CEOs.

Although I had actually met some CEOs in Washington, Beverly, I was a bit shy about asking them what the initials meant. Mr. Ambassador finally explained that they stood for Chief Executive Officer. Since your George is the president of his wholly owned muffin shop, why not refer to him as a CEO when you want to impress?

What mystifies me is that all these Profitable Jobs paid hundreds of dollars to stay glued in their chairs past midnight to here Melvin Thistle, Jr. from State, Baron Spitte, the waltzing diplomat, and 11 others, including my own Mr. Ambassador, talk about Multilateral Relations. The subject is not as interesting as you might think, Beverly. It isn't a fancy name for the more sophisticated kind of marriages. Multilateral Relations are for countries, not husbands and wives.

"Wife of" now has learned the most essential thing about these hotel speech-dinners. Always check out the location of the ladies' before taking your seat at the head table. There's usually a lull when the waiters bring around the cold coffee—which is the only time 300 wives of Profitable Jobs can discreetly sneak out to queue up.

I don't know who decided upon the order of speakers. Maybe our country did something wrong that week because Mr. Ambassador was last on the list.

Generally, CEOs and Profitable Jobs behave with decorum during speeches. But after wine, brandy and the 13th speaker (Baron Spitte spoke for 30 minutes about Whither Europe and World Trade) even CEOs want to go home to their beds. The hard-to-see places from the head table, the alcoves and back rows, were already streaming out the door.

Well, Mr. Ambassador was pretty reluctant to get up and talk about Whither Canada and World Trade. But the Organizer pulled him up by his black tie and intimated that he had better earn his dinner. (Ambassadors go in for this barter system; they eat for free if they give a speech.)

Mr. Ambassador was not in a good mood. Those who had remained were standing and talking while he was. When he sat down there was nobody in the room except me and a few stragglers putting on their coats. The Organizer said, "Next year, we'll have fewer speakers," which was pretty cold comfort.

Since I was one of the very few who had stayed to listen to Mr. Ambassador's speech, I was pretty tired when we returned to the Pierre. The last words I heard from him before I went to sleep were, "Thistle Jr. from State is in the next room."

Thistle had been the first speaker at the banquet.

About four in the morning, Mr. Ambassador shook me awake and I noticed two things. He was fully dressed in his black-tie outfit and there was another man in the room. After a closer look, I realized the stranger was a bellman who was putting our clothes on a rolling rack. I was surprised because checkout time is usually at noon.

"Don't you hear it?" Mr. Ambassador said. "How can you sleep?" Now that I was half-awake, I did hear a moaning, wheezing sound coming from Thistle Jr.'s room.

"Should we call a doctor?" I asked.

"Don't be silly. He's not sick. He's snoring. We're changing rooms.

Mr. Ambassador had already called the bellman while I was still sleeping.

He proceeded first, in his black tie and patent shoes, the bellman following him with the rolling rack, and I walked barefoot behind the bellman, wearing one of those short towel-robes that you're not supposed to steal from hotel rooms. I know what you're thinking, Beverly, but I didn't believe anyone else would be roaming about the 15th floor of the Pierre that time of night.

Our Indian file (squaw last) reached the opening elevator doors just as Sonny Goldstone walked out. You remember Sonny Goldstone, the Gilded Bachelor and Social Asset. He was dressed in white tie, and his girlfriend, Meredith, was wearing a cocktail hat, no less. Mr. Ambassador and Sonny fell upon each other like Dr. Livingstone and Stanley.

They chatted about everything from multilateral relations to which is the "in" nightclub in New York this month. Sonny knows a lot about the latter. Why Mr. Ambassador was interested, I couldn't imagine, because he hasn't been to a nightclub since they closed The Empty Jug in Gravelbourg, Saskatchewan, 35 years ago.

I guess Meredith and Sonny thought the best tactic was to ignore the person standing behind the rolling rack, hugging the Colgate and the Ban and other toiletries close to her chest. Mr. Ambassador didn't even say "You remember my wife?" In fact, Beverly, the only person who acknowledged my presence was the bellman, who said, "Lady, you've dropped the toothbrushes on the floor."

After much joshing and handshaking with Mr. Ambassador, they left us. Meredith did give me a sidelong glance as they passed by the rolling clothes rack.

"Sonny's a gentleman," Mr. Ambassador said in the elevator. "Gentlemen never show curiosity. If we had met your friend George, he would have asked what the dickens we were up to."

Your best friend,
Sondra

The Congressional Chili Cook-off and the Potato War

Dear Beverly,

I don't know what you mean when you say that you want to live your life in the fast lane. George's idea of setting up a muffin shop in the mall basement doesn't sound humdrum to me. I think interesting people do buy muffins. And at least you know what you're doing.

You see, I'm not too sure what I'm supposed to do in my official capacity as a wife of Mr. Ambassador. I'm not even sure if my capacity is official. You remember Popsie Tribble, the Washington socialite? Well, Popsie seems to think I'm stamped with purple ink like a government document. "One of your official duties is to promote your country's exports," she said to me.

Uranium, potatoes or asbestos, I wondered. "Should I have a party in honor of light armored vehicles from Southern Ontario?" "Heavy-Duty Goods are Mr. Ambassador's official duties, not yours," Popsie replied. "I assume that's why he gives those speeches about tariffs and why he corners high administration officials at receptions, instead of me. He even talks to congressmen."

Congressmen are not part of Popsie's world. She never invites congressmen to her Georgetown house. "They're not reliable." I don't know whether she was talking about their punctuality, politics or table manners. But, Beverly, they certainly are powerful in Washington. Popsie doesn't understand about Congress people. I think it's because she gets her picture in Woman's Wear Daily and most wives of congressmen don't. Between you and me, Beverly, Popsie is a bit of a snob and she doesn't consider Congress people "in." Actually, I've never met a congressman, woman, or "wife of" who ever heard of Popsie Tribble.

Mr. Ambassador explained to me that it's possible for one congressman to do more damage to us than one president. If the congressman's home state doesn't like our periwinkles or fiddlehead ferns, he'll get Congress to ban them. The trouble is we don't have any votes in the congressmen's constituencies. Which means Congress people don't care that much about foreign countries except when they need ambassadors to judge a Chili Cook-Off. Mr. Ambassador was a judge at a Congressional Chili Cook-Off. He even wore the special fur hat his mother sent him from Winnipeg. I thought it would be a good idea because most of the congressmen, even those from Connecticut, were wearing cowboy hats. The way the contest works, Beverly, is that each congressman who enters the competition must make the chili himself. But one "wife of" was disgruntled when I congratulated her on her husband's chili. "His chili! Who do you think has been in the kitchen all day?" Well, rules are rules, but I still don't think hanky-panky in the Chili Cook-Off merits a congressional investigation. Especially when Mr. Ambassador says he lost his sense of taste after the fifth entry and probably picked the wrong chili as the winner. Actually, there were several ambassadors judging and he thinks a congressman overheard the word heartburn during the ambassadors' secret multilateral consultations. Maybe that's why steel, turnip and timber interests from the home states have more clout than the ambassadors who judged the Chili Cook-Off. But Mr. Ambassador doesn't agree.

Anyhow, I thought I would help him with Congress by taking Potatoes or Turnips out of the Heavy Goods Category and making them part of my official duties. If the Congress can have a Chili Cook-Off, why couldn't we have a

Potato Party? Mr. Ambassador might not have to talk about potatoes to congressmen if they read headlines like "Mashed New Brunswicks Smash Idaho Gems."

The chef who was with us then (that's a key phrase, Beverly — I'll tell you all about the chefs who've streamed in and out of our place soon), wasn't too keen on an all-potato dinner, so I insisted we go with turnips. Truly it was easier B.W. (Before Washington). That's when I did the cooking myself and didn't have to worry about pleasing chefs, although I do agree in retrospect that my all-turnip dinner idea might have been monotonous. Anyhow, while I was thinking about what to do, a chef from Toronto asked if he could fly in and cook a National Food Dinner, for free. He varied the menu slightly with fiddlehead ferns from the Maritimes, Manitoba Goldeye and a Quebec Duck made into hamburgers. We did get some publicity. My picture was in the newspaper staring at the Goldeye which, as you know, Beverly, is a fish. But there were no headlines about Turnips.

I was furious. I must have fed turnips to 40 press people, some of them world-famous columnists, and there wasn't a glimmer of understanding about the problem. Not one of them wrote a word about Ontario Rutabagas, and now I'm told the Turnip War between our countries is fiercer than ever. It makes me feel pretty useless in this town.

I'm not sure that Popsie Tribble isn't right. Turnips belong in Heavy Goods, and from now on I leave them to Mr. Ambassador and High Administration Officials. And I'm going to forget about Congress, until they start putting turnips in their chili, instead of beans.

Be happy, Beverly, that your muffin shop is part of the clear-cut business world of profit and loss. If you're successful I'll promote them from the Embassy. They won't be categorized as Heavy Duty Goods, unless you're using Popsie Tribble's recipe.

Your best friend,
Sondra

A Gentleman-in-Waiting, or Dexter Tribble Becomes a Powerful Job

Dear Beverly,

It's not the ideal time to invite Popsie Tribble on a canoe trip down the Big Moose Rapids. Besides, she's hardly the white-water type. And are you sure that her Dexter, (Choate, Yale Law, Banking) and your George (Saskatoon, B. A. Sociology, mall-basement muffin shop) will get on? Remember that Dexter was a Powerful Job in a previous administration.

Actually, Popsie's been brooding since I've been here because Dexter has been overlooked by this Administration. She kept telling everyone, "Dexter's born to govern." There are a lot of men like Dexter in Powertown, ostensibly happy with their Profitable Jobs but who are really Gentleman-in-Waiting. Waiting for a phone call that will make them Powerful Jobs once more.

Anyway, Popsie's message must have got across to Melvin Thistle Jr. from State or a White House Person. It's all roses for the Tribbles now. Dexter has been made a Roving Ambassador, which means that Popsie stays in Washington (which she wants), while Dexter drops into town for a party every few weeks.

"We get on best together," Popsie says, "when we're a little apart." Beverly, maybe you should try something like that with George.

Popsie stopped by last week wearing her new spring outfit from Halston. She explained to me that she gets her clothes at cost because she's a well-known socialite who's photographed in W and *Town and Country.*

"Have you given any thought to the guest list?" she asked.

"What guest list?"

"The guest list for the dinner party you're giving in honor of Dexter's appointment. As a wife of a foreign ambassador and an old friend, you should have been the first to ask. As it is, there are already five other parties in our honor. And Dexter is leaving soon because he has to inspect Southeast Asia."

I guess, Beverly, she thought Mr. Ambassador and I were dragging our feet, although Dexter's appointment was only announced the day before our conversation.

Fortunately, Popsie wasn't offended by our tardiness and began to tell me who to invite.

"We'll need two Mr. Secretaries and wives of, of course, three key Members of the Senate Committee who are supposed to approve Dexter's appointment, two White House Persons, three Old Families, Melvin Thistle Jr., World-Famous Columnist Lionel Portant, a Network Anchorman from New York, my designer friends, and Henry."

"You know Henry Kissinger?" I asked.

"Not really, but your social secretary needs an internationally famous name to drop, to attract the others. Only a few pushy types will ask if he's actually accepted."

You know, Beverly, I think Popsie was worried about Dexter not being a sufficient drawing card. "Surely," I said, "the people who invited you and Dexter over when he was out of office will come without an internationally famous name."

Popsie pronounced. "Loyalty isn't everything. If they're not Powerful Jobs, put them on hold. After all, their evenings aren't quite so booked. They can fill in at the last minute if Melvin Thistle, Jr. or the Senators drop out. Dexter needs some fresh contacts. Powerful Friends-to-be."

Popsie opened up the Green Book, which is the Social List of Washington. It's made of green felt with gold lettering and comes out every year. Unless you have a Powerful Job or an Old Family Name, you will get dropped from the new edition. At least that's what Popsie told me. The Order of Precedence in the Green Book begins with the White House.

"Let's start at the top," Popsie said.

I was a little worried about what Popsie meant by the "top." So I switched the subject.

"How many people do you think I should invite?"

"Well," Popsie said, "aim for 60 and ask double. Powerful Jobs receive at least 50 invitations a week and some of them won't be able to come because you're so late with the invitations. At least we'll get credit for asking them."

I knew I was in trouble.

"We can't fit 60 for dinner in our Residence, Popsie."

"Of course, you can't. That's why you'll have to rent a heated tent. Spring weather in Washington is unreliable."

"I think I'll have to ask Mr. Ambassador about the heated tent."

Beverly, heated tents are rather pricy, and I wasn't sure that Dexter Tribble was worth our quarterly budget.

"Let me speak to him," Popsie said.

Well, you know Popsie and her convincing ways. Mr. Ambassador had been traveling a lot and was too polite or too tired to argue with Popsie. We rented the heated tent and asked all the people Popsie suggested.

The dinner is next week, but Henry, Oscar, Halston, Lionel Portant, Thistle Jr., White House Persons, Senators, Mr. Secretaries and even the Old Families haven't yet replied. It's ironic, Beverly. Popsie's old friends are still on our hold list and all the Powerful Jobs have put us on their hold list. Mr. Ambassador says so far as he can tell, the whole party seems to be on hold.

We've only had three acceptances: Joe Promisall, Washington's most expensive lobbyist, and two Profitable Jobs (with wives of), who are also Gentlemen-in-Waiting. I suppose they've accepted because they hope a White House Person will tap them on the shoulder at our dinner.

Forget about the canoe trip, Beverly, and come to our Washington party instead. Things are going so badly, there will certainly be room for you and George.

Your best friend,
Sondra

3.
Inspecting the USA

Having a Nervous Breakdown in the Hamptons

Dear Beverly,

To tell the truth, I'd rather visit you and George in that bat-infested cottage of yours on Lake Ontario than return to the Hamptons this summer.

Mr. Ambassador thinks I'll be calmer *chez* Beverly, instead of having a nervous breakdown in the Hamptons, which happened to me last year.

It was Sonny Goldstone who invited us. He promised a quiet weekend at his "shack" in the Hamptons, far from Powerful Jobs and Head Tables. "Just beer and beach," he repeated. "Beer and beach."

Beverly, I haven't told you about Sonny yet. Popsie says, "If you can't be President, the next best thing is to be Sonny Goldstone."

Admittedly he's a bit of a names-and-planes type. I never know what to say when Sonny mentions he just flew in from lunch with Ceausescu of Romania on Armand Hammer's private plane.

Anyway, Sonny goes to all the best places. Popsie says, "If Sonny's wise, he'll never marry. There will be far fewer invitations once the hostesses have to worry about a 'wife of.'"

I didn't know much about the Hamptons, except that Popsie toid me, "If you go there, it's not considered chic to stay in a hotel." That word should have warned me, Beverly. "Wife of" was rather pooped out from coping with

Washington chic. In retrospect, I would have stayed on the rails if we had lodged with the nameless at a Marriott Hotel.

We were waiting in the little Hampton airport for Sonny's driver to pick us up when the familiar but never-too-friendly World-Famous Columnist, Lionel Portant, came up and spoke.

"Who are you staying with?"

Not where, Beverly, but who. When we mentioned Sonny Goldstone, Portant seemed to find us interesting for the first time.

"I'm thinking of writing a column about your country," Portant said. "Why is it in such a mess?"

Well, Mr. Ambassador had his work cut out for him on the first day of his vacation.

I decided to drift over to the entrance and watch the chauffeured limousines pick up the rest of the people. Mr. Ambassador finally came out sweating. He was afraid Portant's column would scare away the big investors, and, to make matters worse, Portant's last words were, "If you're getting a lift back to Washington, can I hitch a ride?" Mr. Ambassador had to explain that we were not returning on a private plane.

Beverly, don't feel hurt if I tell you that Sonny's shack is nicer than your cottage. And I didn't have to bring my own sheets. It's really a celebrity mansion. "Cary only rents it to his best friends," Sonny explained.

But I knew the weekend wouldn't go well when Sonny introduced us to Meredith, his girlfriend of the week. She wears a bikini inside the house (not a wattle of cellulite anywhere).

"Meredith," according to Sonny, "only associates with famous men, but refuses to marry them because of her career as an actress-writer. Meredith will introduce you to everyone on the beach. It's the Best Beach in the Hamptons."

Until that moment, Beverly, I thought we were going to take a little sun with the kind of anonymous crowd that Mr.

Ambassador and I usually pass time with on beaches. But as soon as we settled on our blanket, we had to get up and shake hands with "the man who saved New York." We lay down again and I put a towel over my eyes. Then we heard Meredith's voice saying something about a director and his Academy Award-winning picture. There was a fat man looking down at us so we had to rise and shake his hand.

It was exhausting, Beverly, because we only spent five minutes prone that afternoon. The lull came between the movie person and a lady "who gives the only parties in New York worth going to."

"Don't you know any of them?" Meredith asked. "What do ambassadors do?"

She was getting bored with our company and went off to dictate her *roman à clef*. "A New York publisher who has a shack next to Sonny's gave me an $85,000 advance."

Washingtonians, as well as New Yorkers, use the Hamptons as a suburb, Beverly. Lionel Portant, Joe Promisall (Washington's most expensive lobbyist) and Melvin Thistle Jr. from State were all standing on the beach talking animatedly to the Somebodies from New York.

"Lets go and chat them up," Mr. Ambassador said unhappily. "Maybe that's what ambassadors are supposed to do." He was worried about Portant scaring away the big New York investors.

Now I know what Sonny meant when he told us he had access to the Best Beach. Topography has nothing to do with Sonny's assessment. It's demography that counts.

"Wasn't I right?" Sonny asked when we returned. "More Famous Jobs congregate on that beach than anywhere else in the Hamptons. I hope you had a rest because now we have to decide which is the best party to go to tonight."

Later I learned that Sonny never confirms his acceptances until he knows who's going where. Meredith gathers this information during her chats with the celebrities on the Best Beach. Sonny never goes on the beach, Beverly. I think he has to stay in the mansion to telephone people about mergers.

"Our publisher friend asked us to a moonlight picnic," Sonny said, "but I think we should go to the Southampton party, for Mr. Ambassador's sake. The host has asked $5 billion worth of investment bankers. Not all of them read Lionel Portant. If you talk to the right people, maybe somebody will buy Manitoba."

Sonny turned to "wife of." "You won't be bored because they always invite a few movie stars to leaven the crowd."

I had already met a movie star, at a White House reception. I was introduced to Wonder Woman. But you know me, Beverly, I hate name-dropping.

Nobody talked to me at the $5 billion party except Sonny, who kept apologizing because Mr. Ambassador was always stuck in the corner with the Wrong People. Eventually, I went off to the corner and began my nervous breakdown.

When we left Sonny said, "The nice thing about the Hamptons is the way the Famous Jobs connect. I actually acquired a new company last night. Too bad you didn't sell Manitoba. I told you how it would be, guys. Just beer and beach. Beer and beach."

Anyway, Beverly, it's your turn this summer. I really am looking forward to seeing the Worst Beach and some Nobodies.

Your best friend,
Sondra

"Wife of" Meets the Most Interesting People

Dear Beverly,

I haven't written you lately because Mr. Ambassador and "wife of" have been doing some travelling through these United States. At first, I was excited, until I remembered that we're one of the few tourists who've ever gone to Arizona without seeing the Grand Canyon, or Orlando, Florida, and missed Disney World, or Los Angeles and missed Beverly Hills.

The problem is that Mr. Ambassador has a programme and the only places designated for us to visit are airports, the roads to airports, hotels, and banquet halls where Mr. Ambassador makes a speech.

As you can see Beverly, I may not be an expert on what there is to see in Arizona, Florida or California, but I certainly know my way around a hotel bedroom. In fact, I've become pretty fussy on the subject, since I spend so much time in them.

There are a few things I'd like to ask hotel-keepers about the way they organize the rooms.

1. Why are there always three pillows on the bed when two people are sleeping in it? Who's supposed to get the extra pillow? Mr. Ambassador and "wife of" always have a little argument about who gets it before turning off the light. It usually ends with Mr. Ambassador saying, "Tell the maid to bring an extra pillow. I have an early meeting tomorrow, so you can wait up for her."

2. Why does the plug in the bathroom say for razors only? What about my electric rollers? I'm tired of crawling under the television set to find a plug, and curling my hair facing an empty TV screen instead of a mirror.

3. Why are telephones placed on tables far from the bed? It's bad enough having a wakeup call at 5:30 a.m., but it's nightmarish jumping out of bed so early in the morning to shut off the noise.

4. Who makes up the identical fruit baskets which appear in our hotel rooms from coast to coast? Wooden apples, unripe pears and three black bananas. Sometimes there are little bottles of jam but without any crackers.

5. Why do they have such short bathtubs with those strips of no-skid tape which always scratch "wife of's" tenderest parts?

6. Why do they always say there will be a 45-minute wait for cold rolls and weak coffee, otherwise known as the Continental Breakfast? Why are cold rolls and weak coffee called the Continental Breakfast?

Beverly, hotel accommodations have become a paradoxical vexation for Mr. Ambassador and "wife of". Sometimes we are given a suite, with real champagne and Godiva chocolates, but only if we're staying for half a day. If we actually are booked for three days, you can be sure we'll find ourselves in the three-pillow broom closet.

Anyway, on our first trip, after an exhausting 10-day voyage from one small hotel bedroom to another, I found that someone had put us in an elegant Oriental suite in the Clift Hotel in San Francisco. It was a one-night stand of course. Nevertheless, a sense of housewifely order came over "wife of" when I saw all that space, and I decided to wash our laundry which had been collecting in the bottom of our luggage for the last week and a half.

I assumed Mr. Ambassador was meeting Governor Jerry Brown in the Governor's office somewhere in San Francisco. (I stopped reading our programme after the fourth day.)

So I put on one of those terry cloth bathrobes, padded around in my bare feet, and draped stockings and underwear over the handsome yellow Chinese chairs in the sitting room. In retrospect, Beverly, I should have shoved all the dirty clothes in the laundry bag and given it to the bellman but I do have my financial quirks. I'd rather order up room service for a party of eight than pay a hotel to wash my stockings.

Just as I was spreading the last nightgown over the air conditioner, there was a knock at the door. Two Secret Service men, Governor Brown, and the hotel manager stared at me.

"Who are you?" they said. "We're here to meet the Ambassador."

Almost at the same moment, Mr. Ambassador veered around the corner with his people. He looked at the room and hissed in my ear.

"Get rid of that stuff and go to the bedroom. Our meeting is in this room. Didn't you read the programme?"

As gracefully as possible, I swept up the laundry and locked myself in the bedroom. But that wasn't good enough for Mr. Ambassador. He came in and told me to put on high heels and a dress.

"Just greet the Governor and then go back in the bedroom."

I dressed, said hello to the Governor and returned to the bedroom. It was two hours before they left. It wasn't worth my life to turn on the TV and interrupt their laughing and joking. And I had left my book in the sitting room. You might say that "wife of" gets to meet the most interesting people.

That's what being an ambassador's wife is like, I guess.

Your best friend,
Sondra

Popsie Tribble and "Wife of" Attend a Political Convention

Dear Beverly,

I was really looking forward to being in San Francisco to observe the Democratic Convention until I met Popsie Tribble, the Washington socialite, on the airplane coming in. She was sitting in the first-class section flipping a Rolodex.

"Invitations, invitations," she sighed. "I've been invited to 47 parties in the next three days and this is the only way I can keep order. That's what political conventions are like."

Well, Beverly, I have to admit I was shocked and a little disgruntled as Mr. Ambassador and "wife of" claimed our seats in the tourist section. We thought we were going to San Francisco for serious business—to watch the American political process in action. Mr. Ambassador did say we might lighten our routine with some extracurricular activities. He promised to take me to the gay-lesbian parade so I could get a glimpse of the Little Sisters of Perpetual Indulgence. (That, Beverly, was the extent of our social commitments.)

I saw Popsie again at the baggage carousel at San Francisco Airport when we arrived. She had to hang around a long time because she brought a lot of luggage with her. "You never know what to wear here with all these micro-climates. I've been asked to dine in Pacific Heights and in Marin County. Hot, cold, hot, cold. I've brought everything from *crepe de Chine* to my marabou cape."

"Are you a delegate?" I asked.

"Heavens no," Popsie said. "I keep out of politics completely, although my Dexter's a roving ambassador in the Republican administration. Of course, he's close to a close-to-a-candidate at the Democratic Convention."

"So I suppose you go to parties to meet the delegates?" I asked.

"Delegates don't go to parties," Popsie replied. "They have meetings in hotel rooms about platforms and worry about who's going to be governor of their states. I wouldn't want to go around holding a sign on the floor of the convention. Anyway, the hall is much too crowded."

"Sometimes," Popsie said dismissively, "the 'wives of' delegates do get to go on a wine tour. But that's because they are not invited anywhere else."

Actually, Beverly, I had been thinking of going on a wine tour myself until that moment. I had no idea that the social life surrounding the convention would be sufficiently substantial to bring a *haute*-party connoisseur like Popsie all the way from Washington. I should have known when I saw all that Vuitton luggage at the airport that the convention is as much a magnet for famous names as the Cannes Film Festival.

"What party are you going to tonight?" Popsie asked me.

"Mr. Ambassador thought we'd have a quiet dinner on our own in China Town."

Popsie was horrified.

"Haven't you been invited anywhere?"

Beverly, until my conversations with Popsie, I had been a happy "wife of." I was planning to see the candidates in the flesh and hear them speak. I was looking forward to taking a trolley car and looking at the pre-earthquake multicolored Victorian houses. I was even going to Alcatraz. You can't imagine the humiliation and anxiety I felt when I told Popsie my plans.

"Trolley cars! Architecture! It's not the outside of the houses you must see, it's the inside."

Popsie pulled out her card index.

"I'll tell you what," she said. "Taxis are hard to get, and I see you have a car waiting for you. If you drive me around I'll get you into some of the parties."

Popsie was as good as her word. We ate cold pasta in plazas and gallerias, and drank free California champagne in hotel rotundas. I dropped two half-eaten sushi in an antique pot at a party at Gump's department store.

Popsie was disturbing to be with. She kept looking beyond me, saying, "Where are the top-echelon people?"

"What do you mean 'top-echelon people'?" I asked.

"Really 'close-to's' the candidate," she answered. "Two 'close-to's' promised to take me out for a private dinner afterward. They left messages for me at the hotel. That's how you find out what's really happening at this convention."

I pointed out a "close-to" Cranston but that didn't satisfy Popsie. There was also a "close-to" Reagan, but somehow even I knew that didn't count at a Democratic convention. All I could see were world-famous columnists and media stars talking to each other. The ratio of media to politicians, Beverly, was 5-to-1.

I finally gave up on parties and went on a wine tour, but I didn't tell Popsie. Baron Spitte, the dusty diplomat, told me that he saw Popsie disappear definitively into a marble mansion in Pacific Heights. She gave up on the convention and went to a fat farm near Los Angeles because she ate too much warmed goat cheese, a California specialty.

I know she expects to be at the Republican Convention. She's keeping a separate Rolodex for Dallas.

Your best friend,
Sondra

Powerful Jobs Attend a Fashion Show

Dear Beverly,

It's been three years since Popsie Tribble went north to visit you, and she's still vexed. She dropped by a while ago, looked at the maple leaf design on our floor and said sourly, "When I think Canada, I think drab. I think galoshes."

Beverly, it's not your fault that she forgot to bring boots and ruined her Maude Frizon sandals, teetering her way on the ice and snow to your front door. Was that when you and George were trial-separating, or was he just too lazy to shovel the walk?

Anyway, Popsie's got a tongue in her head and was going around Powertown whispering, "Canada," "galoshes," "drab" to every "wife of" Powerful Job, which didn't make things easier for Mr. Ambassador and me. I knew we had to counterattack with glamour, so I decided to give a fashion show.

When Popsie heard about it she said, "Of course it will be a ladies' lunch."

"No," I answered. "It's going to be a dinner, with dancing."

Popsie shook her head.

"The men won't come. Powerful Jobs don't go to Fashion Shows. You'll get a hundred women dressed to kill without their Profitable and Powerful Husbands. Do you want my advice?"

I did and I didn't, Beverly. You know how anxious I get after a chat with Popsie.

Popsie continued, not noticing the ambiguous expression on my face.

"Invite everyone for a dinner-dance but don't mention Fashion Show. Once they're all seated, you can throw in the models between soup and the dessert."

When I told Mr. Ambassador what Popsie advised, he said it wouldn't be honorable to ask Powerful Jobs for dinner without telling them about the Fashion Show. So I tested the waters with truthful phone calls and the refusals were instant and diverse. The list our social secretary typed out for us looked something like this:

Popsie Tribble. Washington socialite. Regrets. Conflict. Giving a party the same night for the World-Famous Columnist, Lionel Portant.

(I was angry, Beverly, for two contradictory reasons. Why was she giving a party for Lionel Portant when she knew I was going to ask her and the Portants to my Fashion Show? And why didn't she ask me to her party for Lionel Portant?)

Lionel Portant. World-Famous Columnist and Media Personality. Regrets. Conflict. Speaking in Tampa. (Speaking in Tampa? What about Popsie's party?)"

Congressman Otterbach. Regrets. Conflict. Going to a fish fry. (Congressmen only go to fish fries and chili cook-offs, never ordinary parties. Mind you, Beverly, one "wife of" Congressman told me her husband would go anywhere, even a Canadian fashion show, if I guaranteed the presence of two registered voters from his state.)

Joe Promisall. Washington's most expensive Lobbyist. Regrets. Conflict. High blood pressure. (I wasn't sure how to interpret that one. Should "wife of" call approachable Joe and ask about his health? Or was the idea of a fashion show enough to give him high blood pressure?)

Melvin Thistle, Jr., from State. Regrets. Conflict. Speaking in Tampa.

Baron Spitte. The waltzing diplomat. Regrets. Conflict. Having a physical. (Who has physicals at dinner time?)

Sonny Goldstone. Social Asset and Gilded Bachelor. Regrets. Conflict. Has to meet mother at airport. (Highly suspicious. Sonny Goldstone never meets anyone at airports. He sends limousines. Didn't ever hear him mention a mother.)

Senator Pod. Regrets. Conflict. Speaking in Tampa.

Well, Beverly, I had to do something drastic; 50 fur coats, 16 live models and 30 evening gowns were making their way, as Popsie remarked, "by dog sled" from the north. Naturally we wanted a few photographers and fashion writers especially from New York to publicize the fact that Popsie was wrong about galoshes, Canada and drab.

But to be blunt, sometimes being "wife of" an ambassador makes one cynical. The fashion media would only come if I guaranteed the presence of famous names, like Sonny Goldstone, Senator Pod, Melvin Thistle, Jr. from State, Baron Spitte, and, even worse, Popsie Tribble. I tell you, Beverly, the models could have worn galoshes with the evening dresses, as long as there were Powerful and Profitable Jobs for the fashion media to stare at.

Well, Mr. Ambassador was away speaking in Tampa, so I decided to lie. Without mentioning the words fashion show, I re-invited the Powerful Jobs to something called a dinner-dance extravaganza. It worked like a charm, Beverly; the new list looked like this.

Senator Pod. Accepts. Speech in Tampa canceled.

Lionel Portant. Accepts. Speech in Tampa canceled.

Popsie Tribble. Accepts. Party for Lionel Portant postponed because Portant had to give a speech in Tampa that night.

Sonny Goldstone. Accepts. Mother dead. Not necessary to meet her at airport.

Joe Promisall. Accepts. Blood pressure dropped. Doctor advises exercise, like dancing.

Baron Spitte. Accepts. Very sorry about initial refusal because of physical. His social secretary and nephew, Prince Kiki, got a.m. and p.m. mixed up.

The fashion show went pretty well, considering the fact the temperature was almost a 101 and one of the models wearing a full-length racoon coat (with a hood) fainted right in Congressman Otterbach's lap. A photographer snapped that one, and the papers in Otterbach's home state gave the picture decent play.

Senator Pod left as soon as the models appeared, saying he had to go back to Congress for a vote, although I didn't hear his beeper go off. Melvin Thistle of State left too, muttering something about the Strait of Hormuz. But, Beverly, the rest of the Powerful Jobs reacted to the surprise fashion show with gentlemanly stoicism, I'm happy to say. And best of all, Popsie Tribble was really impressed. I overheard her haggling with one of our fur designers over the price of the full-length raccoon coat.

Your best friend,
Sondra

Houseguest Anxiety

Dear Beverly,

I don't blame you for shutting up the muffin shop these last two weeks in August and resting at the lake. You say it's so empty in the shopping mall George can hear a raisin drop.

It's slow time in Powertown as well. Baron Spitte, the dusty diplomat, has been taking a two-month cure in Baden-Baden. Lionel Portant, the world-famous columnist and media star, is with his kind in Martha's Vineyard. Sonny Goldstone, the gilded bachelor and social asset, asked us to go sailing with him in Newport. But you know me and boats, Beverly. I get seasick on the Potomac 100 yards from the Kennedy Center.

I'm not surprised you haven't asked us to the cottage this year, since Mr. Ambassador and I weren't the easiest of house guests last time. But Beverly, it's hard to be a house guest, no matter whom you are staying with. For instance, I've just come back from Southampton. Popsie Tribble rented a house ($25,000 for six weeks) with four guest bedrooms and servants (which come extra). I think she was as glad to get rid of us as you were. Melvin Thistle, Jr. from State was there at the same time and he left a day early to visit his mother-in-law in Grand Forks, North Dakota.

Your setup by the lake is not the same as Popsie's, of course. It was just like being with family, sharing your bathroom and not having servants around that you have to tip. I told you a hundred times that Mr. Ambassador didn't mind shaving over the little sink in the outhouse where George cleans his bass. Admit it, Beverly, you said before we came that you had no room for a lot of luggage and that hanging space was nil. That's why I didn't bring any sweaters, rubber boots or rain capes. It's just too bad the weather changed the day we arrived. But you and George made up for the cold and rainy weather by letting us wear your woolen clothes. Did you ever remove the wine stain I made on your blue cashmere sweater? The reason we slept past breakfast was because the bat kept frolicking over our heads 'til sunrise. Well, I guess you and George are used to the squeaking and swooping.

As you can imagine, being Popsie's house guests entails a different set of problems, but the anxiety is the same. When we arrived at Popsie's she already looked distraught.

"Gilbert Fry just called to say he can't stay the weekend. It's only you and the Thistles," she said.

Well, you know who Gilbert Fry is, Beverly. The famous author-playwright, and coup for any hostess.

Popsie continued, "The dinner is going to be a flop tonight. Two couples already cancelled when they heard he wasn't coming."

Obviously Mr. Ambassador and "wife of" were not a big enough draw to prevent Popsie's social base from slipping.

Knowing Popsie and her entertaining, I brought everything I owned. Four bags for three days must have been overdoing it because Popsie looked at the luggage and said, "How long did you say you were staying?"

Well, of course it happened. House guest anxiety was upon me. Beverly, here are some of the symptoms:

1. Worrying that the hostess might think that we are settling in for a week instead of a weekend because we brought too much luggage.

2. Being irritated because I leave all my nice clothes in the closet and wear dirty jeans for three days after our hostess says, "We wear pants in this part of Southampton."

3. Being confused about using the half-finished shampoo, toothpaste and Valium left in the medicine cabinet of our bathroom. Were they put here expressly for Mr. Ambassador and me? Or does Popsie sleep here when she

doesn't have house guests? Some people measure the level of their shampoo bottle the way others measure their Scotch. No, Popsie didn't leave any Scotch in our room, but no matter, Mr. Ambassador always brings his own.

(This causes more houseguest anxiety. What does the maid who cleans the room think of the brewery sitting beside the cosmetic bags?)

4. Worrying about the maid brings out house guest anxiety over tipping. There are four servants in the house (if you include the yard man) and we are staying three days. Do we give the money to one of the maids or to Popsie? Will the maid share it with the others? Will Popsie share it with the others? Is there enough to share? (Mr. Ambassador says that staying with Popsie for a weekend is not exactly a freebie. After calculating the travel costs, the house present and the tips, he thought we might have done better at The Pierre in New York.)

5. Worrying about where to put ourselves when we're not sleeping. Our bedroom is upstairs. If we come down to the living room, will we disturb Dexter, who's talking long distance on the phone? There are three lounge chairs outdoors on the patio—but there are four house guests and the Tribbles. If we use up two chairs, where will the Thistles sit? (I still haven't seen the Thistles, but Popsie says they have arrived. Perhaps they are avoiding us. Mr. Ambassador says that Thistle is drinking in the bedroom.)

6. Worrying about arriving at the right time for the party. What's left of the dinner party is supposed to arrive at 8 p.m. Popsie asks us for "an early drink at 7:30." We arrive promptly at 7:30 and I can hear Popsie talking about tennis in the telephone in her bedroom, obviously in no hurry to come downstairs. Dexter has gone to get some ice, and the Thistles are still not for viewing. Mr. Ambassador goes upstairs for his Scotch. The next night we come fashionably late. The outside guests have arrived, wearing silk dresses. I'm wearing blue jeans but cannot return to my room to change as I have been sighted by everyone.

7. Worrying about overstaying our visit. I thought my timing was right until the Thistles left a day early. Popsie said, "You staying on? I thought you were leaving the same time as the Thistles."

Well, Beverly, my house guest anxiety is over for this year and probably the next. I'm not expecting any more invitations.

Your best friend,
Sondra

Cold Pasta
and Politics

Dear Beverly,

To tell you truth, I'm not surprised to hear you put on a few pounds this summer. When George brought the new ice-cream maker and ravioli machine to test at the lake, I knew how it would be.

If it's any comfort, I'll tell you what happened to me. We dined on black pasta and wild mushrooms within a mile of the Golden Gate Bridge, and glazed quail and chocolate mud pie on the 48th floor of a Dallas skyscraper. No, Mr. Ambassador and "wife of" did not deliberately choose to go on a gourmet tour of the United States. We merely attended the Democratic and Republican conventions.

At Gumps in San Francisco and Neiman Marcus in Dallas we bumped into Lionel Portant, World-Famous Columnist and Media Personality, consuming a baby spare rib and a glass of champagne. Normally, you're not supposed to eat in department stores, but this was special because the Democrats and Republicans thought that a cocktail party among the coat racks might be something to remember. At the Dallas department store party, Mr. Ambassador asked Portant for his overview (that's the word he used, Beverly) of the two conventions. Portant, as usual, took his time before answering, mentally sorting out what he should reveal to Mr. Ambassador and what should be held back for the column. Finally he said:

"The sashimi was better at the Democrats but the Republicans know their nachos."

Well, Portant wasn't giving anything away that Mr. Ambassador didn't know already so he left me to talk to Popsie Tribble, whom we last saw in San Francisco at a Democratic cold-noodle party. She was now standing beside the Republican noodle table. (Beverly, there seems to be some connection between cold pasta and politics but I haven't yet figured it out.)

Anyway, I was left with Lionel Portant, who realized he couldn't escape from "wife of" without a polite remark.

"Tell me," he asked, "what do wives of Ambassadors do at American political conventions?"

It was a good question, Beverly, and he wasn't the first to be puzzled. In Dallas, I found myself at a luncheon table where everybody else seemed to be a delegate from Nebraska and nobody including myself knew why I was there. I tried to get into the Nebraska swing of things during the lunch, but my companions weren't fooled, especially when I laughed at Joan Rivers' jokes and the Nebraskans didn't. They were kind enough to include me in a group photo for an Omaha newspaper, but I think I was identified as the Nebraskan-Manitoban delegate to the conventions.

Don't worry, Beverly. That kind of mixup didn't happen too often. In San Francisco and Dallas, the Democrats and Republicans found it safest to entertain neutral diplomats in neutral surroundings like art galleries, where the delegates never go.

Of course, Popsie Tribble is in quite a different category. She attends both conventions because of all the "in parties" she's obliged to go to, the kind that are never mentioned in the newspapers. Popsie's not the only member of the W contingent, dressed in Galanos and Givenchy, who made appearances at the two conventions with invitations filed in Rolodexes. But Popsie, being a Washingtonian, has to be more sensitive to the political aspect of election year. Now she's planning her pre-November entertaining and she told me a little about her difficulties.

"I hope the polls aren't going to be volatile, because I ask my Close-to-the-Candidates in proportion to the latest Harris and Gallup polls. Of course I always use the independent pollsters." Popsie knows Close-to-Mondales, Close-to-Reagans, and even one Close-to-Ferraro.

"But you see," Popsie said, "my invitations have to be out at least four weeks in advance, and if Mondale overtakes Reagan between the acceptance and the party, won't I look like a fool?"

Beverly, I can tell you one thing. Entertainment plans at our embassy are not as muddled as Popsie's, although election year in the States produces rather a suspicious attitude on the part of Powertown towards Mr. Ambassador and "wife of." Important Jobs seem to think we smile wider at the Close-to whose candidate goes up in the polls. But embassies don't operate like Popsie Tribble.

Congressman Otterbach, D., said to me rather acidly,

"If Mondale doesn't get in I suppose you won't have me for supper."

Congressman Otterbach has had something to do with quotas on Heavy Goods (hogs and steel, Beverly, hogs and steel) for the last 20 years and will continue to do so for the next 20. (Mr. Ambassador told me 90 percent of all Congressmen get reelected no matter who becomes President.)

Now Congressman Otterbach gets overwrought during the pre-election session and begins to toy around with tariffs.

So Mr. Ambassador smiles very wide at Congressman Otterbach and tells him to name the day he wishes to dine. Well, of course, Otterbach is always speaking in Tampa and Atlanta when he's not in congressional session, but says he might drop in after his election.

Anyway, Beverly, good luck with the club soda and salad diet. I'm on Tab and toast myself.

Your best friend,
Sondra

4.
Tribal Customs
in the USA

Sonny Goldstone's Celebrity File

Dear Beverly,

I'm sorry you envy "wife of" and Mr. Ambassador because we've been to five cities in a month. Admittedly our life seems richer than yours, but traveling the way we do has some low moments. When you spend only a brief time in each city it's like interrupting a conversation on a subject you know nothing about.

As far as I can judge, we travel because Mr. Ambassador has to make a speech, meet the governor, throw a ball or drop a puck. For reasons of state he occasionally has to combine the sports event with the speeches, and we both find this so nerve-racking that we forget about Sonny Goldstone's file.

Unlike Mr. Ambassador and "wife of," Sonny, the Social Asset and Gilded Bachelor, knows how to travel. Hotels are important to Sonny. He says, "There's nothing I love more than walking into the Beverly Hills in Los Angeles after putting a big deal together." His personal file contains lists of the best hotels, the best restaurants and members of the Forbes Four Hundred in every major city. (Those are the 400 richest people in the United States, Beverly.)

He also updates his file with the latest local scandal so he'll be in the know when he hits Chicago, Los Angeles or Atlanta. But even though Sonny is generous about sharing his file, we've never been able to take advantage of it.

When we returned from Dallas, Sonny asked, "Did you stay at the Mansion on Turtle Creek, as I told you?"

"We stayed at the Hilton," I replied. "The Mansion was all filled up. Anyway, the Hilton was cheaper — only $52 a night, for a double."

"I chalk that up as a loss for your country," Sonny said. "What sort of impression can an ambassador make in Dallas by staying at a cheap hotel? What did Trammell Crowe say when you told him where you were staying?" (I think, Beverly, that Trammell Crowe is a person on the Forbes list.)

"He didn't say anything," I replied, "because we never called him up."

"I can see why you went to New Orleans," Sonny said. "Nobody on the Forbes list lives there. Relieves the pressure on Mr. Ambassador, I guess. Where did you stay?"

"A nice little place in the French Quarter. We even had a suite with a fruit basket." I hoped that would mollify him.

"When I go to New Orleans," Sonny said, "I always stay at the Royal Pontchartrain. Just because it's not in the French Quarter, which, of course, is too touristy. In any case, hotels in New Orleans aren't as important as restaurants. Did you eat at Moscas?"

"No, we ate in our hotel room. We didn't have time because of the speeches."

Sonny was horrified.

"Nobody eats in his hotel room in New Orleans, even if he has a free fruit basket. To whom did he speak?"

"It was Canada Night at the World's Fair," I said, "and there was an audience of 3,000 waiting for the dancers to come on. Mr. Ambassador had to speak before the show."

"I hope he didn't share any heavy political thoughts with a group waiting for a little light entertainment."

"He mentioned acid rain," I said, a little weakly. "But he only spoke for five minutes, and I don't think the microphone was working."

"Be thankful for that," Sonny concluded. "When you went to Chicago, did you call on the Pritzkers?"

"Who are the Pritzkers?"

Sonny was beside himself. "Five hundred million dollars
each on the Forbes list. Probably more. Real estate, timber,
hotels. Chicago's a money town. Why on earth would anyone go there unless it was to make a deal." Then Sonny had
a thought. "I also gave you Saul Bellow's number in case
Mr. Ambassador's business was cultural."

"We didn't call anybody," I said, "because Mr. Ambassador spent most of his time in the dugout waiting to throw the
ball. It was the opening game of the season between the
Chicago Cubs and the Montreal Expos. They are baseball
teams," I added.

Sonny said, "I know that. What happened?"

"First we listened to the two national anthems, then the
mayor spoke, then they called out the names of the ball-
players and finally they mentioned Mr. Ambassador's
name. And then it started to rain. Everybody waited for an
hour, but it rained so hard they had to cancel the game. Mr.
Ambassador never got to throw out the ball. But he caught a
cold."

"That's too bad," Sonny sympathized.

"No, it isn't," I said. "I remember what happened in San
Francisco. Mr. Ambassador threw the ball at the opening
game of the San Francisco Giants and the Expos and it
bounced before it reached the plate. No," I added, before
Sonny could ask the question, "we didn't call Gordon
Getty."

"At least," Sonny said, "you must have done some tour-
ing. Did you drive to Big Sur?"

"Halfway," I said. "But we had to turn back because it
was too foggy to see the road."

"Where did you go after that?"

"The airport. It was the only place where there wasn't
any fog and we had to get back to Washington because Mr.
Ambassador had to drop the puck. The Edmonton Oilers
and the Capitals were having an opening game. They're
hockey teams."

Sonny said, "I know that. Did everything go well?"

"He dropped it on his shoe," I replied. "But they gave him a second chance."

Don't get me wrong, Beverly, our trips are not limited to airport roads, sports stadiums and convention hotels. There's generally a reception at the top of the tallest building. I don't know why it is, but locals seem proudest of the view that is the most remote from their city.

There's also the art gallery reception, but the place where they hang the pictures is roped off. Cocktails and canapés can ruin the canvases. And then there's the obligatory tour of where the rich people live. My knowledge of the Forbes 400 is limited to staring at their hedges from the road.

"You can't really see the house from here," says our well-meaning guide, "but it cost five million and who knows how much has gone into it."

I do know one thing, Beverly. While we're staring from the outside, Sonny Goldstone's inside, closing a deal.

Your best friend,

Sondra

Carnal Passions In Powertown

Dear Beverly,

Frankly, I'm appalled by your letter saying you're fed up with my news of election campaigns and you'd rather know about the latest Washington sex scandals. It's a mistake to think that Powertown rolls them by one after the other. I've been here over two years and would almost guarantee that Washington is a wasteland for the carnal passions. But to satisfy your prurience, Beverly, I dropped in to Popsie Tribble's the other day, who of course leads a less sheltered life than "wife of," living in Georgetown as she does.

"Well," she said, offering me some nicotine chewing gum (Popsie's trying to give up the Balkan Sobranies), "since the business on the steps of Capitol Hill, sex has disappeared as we used to know it. Secret Vice has taken its place."

I was astonished.

"You mean whips...and chains...and..."

"Far too crude for Washington," Popsie said.

"Now take Lionel Portant, World Famous Columnist and Media Star, happily married, four children, a house in the Vineyard. I suppose you don't know about his Secret Vice. When 'wife of' Portant refused to comply, he was forced to go elsewhere, and found a female congressional staffer."

"Comply to what?" I breathed.

"Reading aloud his old columns, and watching video tapes of his appearances on the talk shows. The two of them do this in the afternoon, *entre cinq et sept*, French style. Same old story," Popsie said with a sigh. "She's 20 years younger than 'wife of,' who doesn't even read Portant's new columns. Now don't go telling the world because I wouldn't want his family hurt."

"Why does she do it?" I asked.

"The staffer you mean? She does it for Senator Pod's sake. He's on the Finance Committee and he mistakenly believes that a positive mention from Portant on the tube will help his reelection."

"Why does she do it for Senator Pod?" I asked.

"Ambition," Popsie answered. "She wants to become a Powerful Job and needs his support. I suppose," Popsie said a little ruefully, "you might classify her behavior as sexual instead of political, given the confused libido of Powertown."

I know what you're thinking, Beverly, Popsie Tribble is our age and probably misses out on a lot.

I was lucky enough to bump into Sonny Goldstone, the Social Asset and Gilded Bachelor, who happens to be a yumpie expert. He was coming out of the Jockey Club, after sharing crabcakes with some CEO's.

"Do you young people have any sexual scandals?" I asked, walking with him along Massachusetts Avenue.

"Sex, if it happens among the yumpies, is never a scandal," Sonny said. "Sexual scandal has been replaced by something much more damaging."

"Secret Vice?" I asked.

Sonny shook his head dismissively.

"You see too much of Popsie Tribble. I suppose she told you about that staffer who reads aloud to Portant. Everybody knows, so it's not a secret, and nobody cares, so it's not a vice."

"What about her relationship with Senator Pod?" I asked.

"I suppose you're referring to the time when she went with him on a fact-finding mission to Ochos Rios, investigating resort hotels. Same thing. Everyone knows, nobody cares."

"Not even 'wife of' Pod?" I asked.

"Nobody cares about 'wife of' Pod."

"What do Powerful Jobs care about?" I asked.

"Disclosure," Sonny said.

"You mean there are Powerful Jobs who are flashers?" I was shocked.

"Don't be ridiculous. I'm talking about financial disclosure. It has replaced sex if you're looking for a scandal. The neo-Puritans now peek through bank accounts and tax returns for Conflict of Interest. Believe me, there's nothing more salacious than thinking you've discovered a hidden Conflict of Interest."

"How does someone know when he's practicing Conflict of Interest?" I asked.

"That's the trouble," Sonny replied. "In the old days, a Powerful Job certainly knew when he was practicing illicit sex. It's much harder to figure out if you're practicing Conflict of Interest. You never really know if you're doing it. I must say, it takes the pleasure away."

"I can see why you don't want to go into public office, and expose your conflicts of interest," I said, sympathetically.

"You know," Sonny replied, "I think I could get the habit under control. But it's too late for my mother; she's been practicing it for years. Anyway, don't worry about me. Worry about that staffer who has to fill out the disclosure forms."

"She's going to be exposed?"

"Her father built some sewage plants in the Poconos."

"So what?" I asked.

"I couldn't repeat in polite company what he had to do to get the contract. And you've heard about her brother, the dentist?"

"What's dubious about dentistry?" I asked.

"He put a no-frills nursing home near one of the sewage plants in the Poconos."

"You mean it really smells bad?"

"She hasn't got a chance."

Beverly, I wouldn't go in for double bookkeeping with your muffin shop. George might want to run for Alderman and you'll never get over the shame.

Your best friend,
Sondra

Purposeful Fun
in Powertown

Dear Beverly,

Well I'm sorry you and George have decided that Mr.
Ambassador and "wife of" never have any real fun in
Washington. It's not quite true that we give parties only for
ulterior motives, like promoting light armored vehicles
from Ontario. Admit it, Beverly, our life has to be more
serious than yours, given the importance of Powertown.

Nevertheless, Powerful Jobs must do something for fun in
their idle hours, so I decided to pick Popsie Tribble's brain. I
rang her at 5 in the afternoon, knowing she would just be
back from a champagne tea to which I was not invited. (Karl
Lagerfeld was making a personal appearance.)

"Do you have fun, Popsie," I asked, "in your idle hours?"

"An effective Washington socialite has no idle hours,"
Popsie said reprovingly. "Especially me, remember my
Puritan heritage. What with my yoga lady in the morning
and the lunches at the F Street Club I give for the 'wifes of'
whose husbands might be useful to Dexter, I barely have the
strength to attend the gala charity balls at night. You know I
never stay for the dancing."

"But," I said, "wife of Thistle Jr. from State told me she
and Melvin found boat parties on the Potomac very
relaxing."

"I was invited to one just last week," Popsie replied. "The
host ticked me off because I was wearing Charles Jourdan
pumps instead of some footwear called topsiders. We had to
wait an hour for Congressman Otterbach before we could set
sail, or whatever boats do when they move. My Dexter had

to leave for Bangkok the next morning at 6. Very irritating. All the Powerful Jobs on the boat (the guest list, at least, was satisfactory) agreed that a Congressman should never keep a Roving Ambassador like Dexter waiting. It was a real breach of status. We got even with Otterbach by taking the best seats on the deck and making him sit downstairs where there's no air-conditioning."

"Was the view on the deck nice?"

"Well, we went by that sewage plant on the Potomac. It's the first time I've had a close look at it in 30 years."

"Anyhow," I said, "with all those powerful jobs on board, the conversation must have been fascinating."

"There was no conversation because of the noise," Popsie replied.

"What noise?"

"The noise from the planes taking off and landing at National Airport."

"I suppose," Popsie added, "boats can be fun for those who like being in a Winnebago on water. But not for Popsie Tribble."

Popsie continued, "If you really want to know what people do in their idle time, why don't you ask Baron Spitte, the dusty diplomat? He's got plenty of it."

Although it was siesta time in the Baron's residence, he graciously received me in his paisley dressing gown which he keeps handy in case of the unexpected afternoon caller.

"Your friend Beverly," the Baron agreed, "has put her finger on something. There is no such thing as simple fun in Washington. Fun must be purposeful. Take tennis, for instance. When Melvin Thistle from State plays tennis with Senator Pod (who's trying to block his new appointment) Thistle Jr. marks down his tennis errors in a little book. And then he studies it in his idle time."

"Does that improve his game?" I asked.

"I think it improves Pod's game. He's never going to let Thistle's appointment pass through the Senate."

"What does Sonny Goldstone, the Gilded Bachelor and Social Asset, do in his idle time?" I wanted to know.

"Sonny jogs. Right after he finishes his crab cakes at the Jockey Club. His chauffeur follows him slowly down the Mall and, when he finishes his 40 minutes, Sonny changes clothes in the limousine while talking about mergers on his new cellular phone."

"Do you think my friend Beverly is right when she says our dinners always have ulterior motives?"

"What can we poor ambassadors do?" the Baron said. "Powerful Jobs don't like coming to embassy parties for mere conviviality. Remember my rule about entertainment. You must know it by now."

"Which rule is that?"

"Never have dancing unless the party is in honor of a charity. Powerful Jobs will forgive the fact that a band might strike up after dinner if the phrase 'Charity Ball' is tacked on to the invitation. The phrase prevents your guests from appearing frivolous if their names get in the papers. Washingtonians will only dance for a worthy cause."

The Baron continued wistfully:

"Once I forgot myself and gave a dinner dance for no reason at all. The few people who accepted bolted down their food and left as soon as the band began to play. The only guests on the floor dancing to the five-piece orchestra were a Used-To-Be-Close-to a forgotten candidate and a former Mr. Secretary from the Truman administration. Of course, they were with their third wives."

I wondered if the Baron did anything just for fun. He smiled when I asked him.

"I believe in solitary pleasures. Having fun with others in Powertown involves too much stress."

The Baron walked me around his Tapestry Room, where he gave that disastrous musicale for the media I wrote you about.

"You see those rugs hanging on the walls? I hooked them all myself."

Well Beverly, it wasn't a totally wasted conversation, because he's promised me one for Christmas.

Your best friend,
Sondra

The Space Shuttle Leaves "Wife of" Behind

Dear Beverly,

I haven't been able to write you lately because "wife of" has been traveling. First time in Cleveland, first time in St. Louis, and first time in Space. Space isn't as scary as you might think, Beverly, because the NASA people ease you up there slowly, making sure that you see something familiar at first, like the Holiday Inn at Cocoa Beach, Fla., with the reassuring strips over the toilet seats and the drinking glasses in sanitized paper. That's where the real astronauts hang out, I'm told, when they're not floating about the upper ionosphere with screwdrivers and pens sticking to their bodies with Velcro tape.

To tell you the truth, I don't think the NASA people had any intention of letting me get too far off the ground once Mr. Ambassador told them I have to be let out of the Buick every half hour (along with the dog) because I get queasy in the back seat. And they realized I wasn't mechanically minded during the indoctrination talks when they told us about simulated satellite values and the difference between cosmic and gamma rays.

Mr. Ambassador said he was embarrassed when I asked them, "I guess you'd be the fellows who'd know where the electric light goes when I turn off the switch?"

He said my question showed I belonged to the Dark Ages of Science, but I think Mr. Ambassador is a bit of a hypocrite because he doesn't know the answer either.

In theory, Beverly, I might have been a good candidate for Space because they are conducting queasy-feeling studies up there. But I didn't want to be part of the program when I heard about their methodology. The way I understand it, the astronaut doctor happens upon another astronaut floating around in the shuttle, who's feeling pretty good till then, even without the gravity. Well, the doctor actually tries to induce my back-seat-of-the-Buick feeling, in the healthy fellow, in the name of queasiness-research. It does make the stomach churn, and I'd never volunteer.

I suppose you're wondering why I went to Cocoa Beach, Fla., in the first place. Mr. Ambassador was asked to come and watch the space shuttle launch because a Canadian astronaut was part of the crew. It was kind of them to include "wife of" with the rest of the dignitaries, because basically my job at the launch site is the same as it is in Washington.

I'm supposed to step out of the way when they take pictures of the Famous Names.

I don't know whether I've mentioned this camera business to you before, but there's always someone snapping pictures at semi-public events in Powertown and anywhere else where even semi-famous names might appear. Baron Spitte, the waltzing diplomat, says he's never sure to whom the camera belongs. The photographer might be snapping for worldwide coverage and your face could be on the front page of 60 newspapers. (It's never happened to the Baron.) On the other hand, the fancy camera might belong to the father of the host, who wants to get a snap of his son with a Powerful Job to embellish the family scrapbook.

No matter who the cameraman represents, Beverly, he always asks me to step aside so Melvin Thistle, Jr., from State or Dexter Tribble, the Roving Ambassador, can be photographed without me cluttering the picture.

George probably thinks I deliberately hang around
Famous Names just in case the cameraman forgets to ask me
to step aside. Tell George that occasionally I have to get
close to a Powerful Job in order to shake hands in the reception line. And I can tell you it bruises the ego when I hear an
aide whisper to the photographer, "Let her pass before you
take the next shot." Anyway, another reason you didn't see
a picture of me chatting with the astronauts at the space
shuttle launch is that the NASA people realized after my
electric light question that I wouldn't be able to have a
rational conversation about chip hardening and tile
deterioration.

But "wife of" actually did see the launch, and, Beverly,
there's something about the preparations and event that
reminds me of another marvel: the way my Auntie Zora
makes omelettes. Gerald, her husband, is a fussy eater.
Auntie Zora travels miles out of town to buy eggs from a
farmer she can trust. She rises at 3 a.m. to separate the eggs
and let them settle. At 4 a.m. she combines three yolks and
one white and puts them in a martini shaker (six shakes, 30
seconds each). She and the eggs wait one hour, until Uncle
Gerald comes downstairs, for the blast-off, so to speak. The
moment he sits down at the table she throws some butter in
the pan, adds a teaspoon of ketchup to the eggs, and counts
down 20 seconds until they turn into a red and gold sponge.
Gerald always tests the omelette for last-minute malfunc-
tions, probing it with a knife.

I remember him saying, "Sondra, look quickly, if you
want to see a perfect omelette." Then he'd wrap it around
his fork and swallow the whole thing in one gulp.

At Cocoa Beach we rose at 3 a.m., waited around during
the refined preparations, hoping the weather would settle,
and finally went to a special place at 5, where we could feel
the earth tremble when the launch went up. Precisely on

schedule, the marvel appeared, all red and gold, brightening the sky for 60 seconds. It disappeared from sight as quickly as Auntie Zora's omelette.

That's what it was like, Beverly.

Your best friend,
Sondra

A-list and Election Parties

Dear Beverly,

It's a good thing I have you to confide in, because there's something about a conversation with Popsie Tribble that always makes me feel my life is dull and wanting. Mr. Ambassador calls her the "Great Destabilizer" and says that only weak-minded "wives of" pay her so much attention.

Lately, Popsie has been touching base with me by telephone because of her hectic party agenda.

"I'm pooped," she said. "Paris, London, New York, Newport. That's where all the A-list parties have been. Thank heavens for the Concorde."

I tried to switch the subject and told her I thought I was finally getting the hang of Washington.

"Well, that's not hard," she said. "It's such a parochial town. They wear white tie more often even in New Orleans." She paused. "I didn't see you or Mr. Ambassador at any of the A-list parties."

"I don't think they have our names. Who makes up the A list anyhow?" I asked.

Popsie was vague.

"You're either on it or not. It's hard to explain these things. Perhaps it would help if they put you in *Vogue*, W or *Town and Country*. But I don't think that will happen." She spoke as if she knew something.

Well, Beverly, Popsie wasn't telling the whole truth about how she gets asked to parties. I happen to know that she carries a Rolodex with her when she travels, which contains worldwide unlisted numbers. When she arrives in

Paris, let's say, she calls up a medium-important name and says she's come to town to dine alone with a Very Important Name. (No one can really verify if this is true.) Impressed, the medium-important name gives a party in her honor and Popsie's out-of-town social life begins.

Popsie continued:

"It was a lot of fun but I had to come back for the presidential debates and the election."

Beverly, I thought Mr. Ambassador was wrong; Popsie does have a serious side.

"What did you think of the debates?"

"I hate eating off trays."

"Trays?" I asked.

"They make you eat off trays at debate parties because you have to watch the television. 'Wife of' Portant was silly enough to serve soup, and I spilled it on my Missoni balloon pants. They're 10 years old but good enough for debate parties. It's a very uncivilized way to entertain. Actually I gave a little party in honor of the last debate. Very small, only 'Close-to-the Candidates' as guests, and no trays."

"How did it go?" I asked.

"Not terribly well," Popsie admitted. "We nearly missed the debate. I forgot it was on an hour early, because of Kansas Time. The 'Close-to's' rushed to the television and refused to come into the dining room at all. So nobody ate; and then they began to fight over the gonger."

"What's a gonger?"

"You know, the remote control thing that switches channels. The Close-to's got upset with Dexter, after the debate, when those commentators come on. You see, Dexter's not handy with the gonger. He always gets the commercials. The Close-to's thought he was doing it on purpose because he said he hates it when those commentators tell him what he's supposed to think."

"I suppose you've been invited to a lot of election parties?" I asked.

"Naturally," Popsie replied. "I'd rather go to the intimate chic ones in Georgetown, but then you have to stay all evening or the 'wife of' will be insulted. But I really think Dexter ought to do a walk-through of the Republican and Democratic election parties, just to be seen."

I suppose Popsie's thinking of Dexter's job as Roving Ambassador. I think he wants to be reappointed. Both the Administration and Congress have a hand in Dexter's future, so he can't be too careful.

I know, Beverly, you think that Popsie sounds shallow, but she did put her finger on something about life in Power-town. You have to appear in public from time to time so people know you exist. In Ottawa, you don't have to attend a big party. You just go to the farmers' market on a weekend and see everyone you want. But it's not quite the same here. I tried sitting for an afternoon in Dupont Circle and not one person said hello to me.

I asked Sonny Goldstone, the Gilded Bachelor and Social Asset, if there was a public place in Washington, like an agora, where Powerful Jobs congregate.

"Aside from the tennis courts?"

"Yes."

"Sometimes I hang around the dried-mushroom section at Sutton Place on a Saturday morning. Joe Promisall occasionally drops in to the Georgetown Safeway and claims he's made a few deals. They say it's worth being seen at the Giant Gourmet in McLean, but I think it's a waste of time. Too long a drive from Capitol Hill."

Anyway, Beverly, give my best to the Prime Minister when you see him at the farmers' market next Saturday.

Your best friend,
Sondra

Popsie Tribble's White-Lie Technique

Dear Beverly,

Popsie Tribble came over yesterday, and I must say she was in a fretful mood. She's even given up her nicotine chewing gum and has reverted to the Balkan Sobranies.

"What are you so nervous about?" I asked. "The election is over, and you don't have to worry about your inauguration ball dress till January. I would have thought you and Dexter would have left Washington during this quiet time to go shooting in Scotland or wherever."

"A lot you know about it," Popsie replied. "Dexter says we entertained the wrong Close-Tos before the election. Not one of them has been heard of since Nov. 6. To make things worse, there's this talk about a new Powerful Job."

"What Powerful Job?"

"They say there's going to be a Czar."

"You mean the Russians are going to reinstate the monarchy?" I must say I was astonished. "Nobody sent Mr. Ambassador a telegram. I think he would have mentioned it to me."

"Don't be silly," Popsie said. "The administration, our administration, is thinking of putting a Czar in charge of the Soviets."

Popsie was talking pretty wildly, Beverly. It sounded as if a splinter group in the Pentagon or the CIA was planning a Kremlin Putsch to replace Chernenko with a Romanoff. "I mean," Popsie said, finally clarifying her thoughts, "they're thinking of putting a Czar in charge of arms control to deal with the Soviets."

"The word," I said, "is confusing, given the context."

"It's nerve-racking not knowing who he might be," Popsie said, ignoring my comment. "I want to invite the Czar to a party."

"Maybe Melvin Thistle, Jr. from State knows something."

"Thistle Jr. isn't talking to us." Popsie paused and added, "Somehow, he has this notion that Dexter is lobbying for his job."

Actually, Beverly, I read that in Lionel Portant's column, but I didn't think it was polite to mention it. "I didn't know that Melvin Thistle, Jr. wanted to quit," I said.

"He doesn't," Popsie said. "That's the trouble."

"I thought Dexter likes being a Roving Ambassador."

"You mean," Popsie said, "a Forgotten Ambassador. I think he was roving too far away from the power center. That's why he guessed wrong about the real Close-Tos at our pre-election parties." Popsie sighed. "Uncertainty is making me look haggard. I am booking myself in for a facial. I have to look my best because the party I'm giving is in honor of the new head of the Foreign Relations Committee. He's the one who has to approve Dexter."

"If Thistle Jr. leaves," I added. "So you know who's going to be the head of the Foreign Relations Committee?" I thought I had a tidbit for Mr. Ambassador.

"That's the trouble, Popsie said. "I don't. They say you have to be in the Senate steam bath to find out the latest in the negotiations."

"Then how do you know who your guest of honor will be?" I asked.

"There are several possible candidates," she said. "I used the traditional Washington white-lie technique. I told each senator the party was in honor of him. By the time I have my party, they should have made up their minds. How long can a senator stay in a steam bath?"

Popsie continued, "I have given many a dinner where at least three Powerful Jobs thought they were the only guest of honor. It's just a matter of clever seating. Of course, Dexter will have to give several after-dinner toasts. Just to fudge things up."

"You shouldn't be nervous," I said. "Your party seems under control."

Popsie disagreed. "Not entirely. First there's the matter of the written invitations. Each senator will have to receive an invitation with his name written on as guest of honor. And it's not only a matter of varying the text of a few invitation cards. When I told each senator that he was my guest of honor, I asked him if there was anyone special he wanted invited."

"That was nice of you," I said.

"It's part of the Washington social bargain," Popsie said. "But this time it's worked against me. The senators wanted members of their staffs invited. And you know how large those Senate staffs can be. And each senator seems to have his chief fund-raiser and 'wife of' visiting from his state on the day of my dinner. They had to be invited. Two senators wanted me to invite their mothers-in-law, who live in Washington, in decent obscurity, but would be hurt if not asked."

"You don't think anyone will compare their invitation cards?" I asked.

"I don't trust those Senate staffers," Popsie brooded.

"How many people are you having?"

"Close to 80. My dining room only seats 24. After all, I live in Georgetown."

"What are you going to do about the Czar?" I wanted to know.

"Invite him of course. But I'm waiting for all the likely names to appear in Portant's column."

"You'll have to rent a tent."

"If I do," Popsie said, "I'll send you and Beverly invitations."

"Why don't you put Beverly's name down as guest of honor on her card?"

"That's an idea." Popsie cheered up. "I'll get some credit, and she probably won't come."

Your best friend,
Sondra

"Wife of"
Attends a
Working Picnic

Dear Beverly,

I don't know what it is, but we've been here a couple of years, and each time July 4th rolls around "wife of" never gets a chance to see the fireworks or even take part in some of the tribal customs.

I had high hopes this year because we arrived back in Washington on time and had received several exclusive invitations. But as usual, things went awry and we weren't able to attend the best of them. Let me tell you what we missed.

1) Dancing by the Sugar Foot Cloggers on Pennsylvania Avenue at the Old Post Office. Congressman Otterbach asked us to accompany him. He was not participating in the dance but a friend of his mother was.

2) An informal picnic (no ties, of course) in Malcolm X Park, where Muhammed Ali was going to speak. Senator Pod, who invited us, said he was bringing along his Rhodesian Ridgeback.

3) A package tour for diplomats from soft currency countries, organized by a colleague of Baron Spitte, to go and eat the free hot dogs at Gaithersburg fairgrounds and then on to JKJ Chevrolet to take advantage of their $1-over-factory-invoice sale. Mr. Ambassador wasn't interested in the free hot dogs because he only likes them split and grilled over mesquite. Baron Spitte said it was an all-or-nothing deal.

4) A combination garage sale and zucchini and sweet potato BBQ organized by "wife of" Lionel Portant. Popsie Tribble said, "Unless you buy one of Portant's old manual typewriters, you don't get to eat."

The reason we didn't attend any of these festivities is because at the very last moment Melvin Thistle, Jr., from State actually asked us to his home for a 4th of July picnic. I told Mr. Ambassador that Congressman Otterbach and the Sugar Foot Cloggers had first priority, but Mr. Ambassador said that Thistle added, "There's something we have to clear up that's been left adrift for too long a time."

Then Thistle Jr. put us into a real panic when he announced, before hanging up the phone, "By the way, Mr. Ambassador, you'd better wear a tie."

Beverly, there are strict rules in Powertown about ties and parties. Men wear white tie to the Gridiron, black tie to Popsie Tribble's dinners and striped, dotted or paisley ties for everything else—except picnics. Picnics are always no-tie affairs; it says so in the Green Book.

Well, at first glance Thistle's back yard looked innocent enough for the 4th of July: the trestle tables offered the traditional fried chicken, potato salad and watermelon, along with little American flags. But the "wives of" had already been pushed to a side huddle when we arrived, and the Powerful Jobs from the Pentagon, the White House and State were all wearing the soberest of ties. Dots only. Now I knew what a "working picnic" meant.

As soon as we managed to choke down some chicken, Thistle Jr. rose and spoke to the assembly.

"Mr. Ambassador," he said, "have you ever read the Declaration of Independence?"

Humiliated, Mr. Ambassador replied, "Regretfully, no."

"Let me read you," Thistle continued, "the part where your country is mentioned."

This came as a shock, Beverly. We had no idea Canada was in the Declaration of Independence. I whispered to Mr. Ambassador that he was really falling down on the job.

Mr. Ambassador told me to shut up because Thistle began to read to the now silent company.

It was hard to understand at first, but finally I heard something like this.

"For abolishing the free system of English Laws in a neighboring Province, establishing therein an arbitrary government..."

Mr. Ambassador said, softly, "Oh, God, that's Quebec."

Thistle went on. And it got even worse.

"...and enlarging the Boundaries so as to render it at once an example and fit instrument for introducing the same absolute rule in these Colonies."

Mr. Ambassador said *sotto voce* to "wife of," "The signers say that we made a land grab from the United States."

That must have been the serious part, Beverly, because the Powerful Jobs seemed less agitated about our rotten behavior over Quebec. But they all exchanged significant glances when Thistle dropped that "enlarging its boundaries" part.

Mr. Ambassador couldn't take it any longer and interrupted undiplomatically. "What is it, Thistle? Are you making territorial demands?"

After a lengthy silence, a White House person spoke. I noticed there were a few watermelon seeds splattered on his tie.

"Ambassador," he said, "Don't you think our grievances must be addressed?"

That's what you call formal diplomatic language, Beverly, which means that nobody really knows what's behind the words. I still don't remember how we escaped, but I can tell you the fried chicken didn't sit too well in Mr. Ambassador's stomach that night. We missed the fireworks again (third time around) because he insisted on sending a telegram immediately to Ottawa.

Beverly, I told him I thought it was all a joke but he said that Thistle's July 4th picnic might have been a subtle hint about things to come. Now there's a lot of paper going back and forth from the embassy to headquarters speculating if, when and where the invasion might take place.

Your best friend,
Sondra

5.
The Domestic Manners of the Americans

Thank-you Notes are a Way of Life

Dear Beverly,

As you know, Popsie Tribble's pronouncements on the social behavior of Washingtonians usually have a depressing effect on "wife of." I forgot to tell you about the one she sprang on me not long after I arrived.

"The best time of the day to write your thank-you notes is in the afternoon, between four and six."

"Thank-you notes for what?" I asked.

"For the lunches, dinners, receptions and teas that you and Mr. Ambassador will have to attend. It's considered the polite thing to do in Washington. I suppose you never heard of the custom where you come from."

Well, Beverly, you know the kind of social life we used to have. George would have choked on his muffins if I sent you a handwritten note for the festivities in honor of your brother, the professor of dentistry, who just published his third book on root canal. Also, I didn't think a thank-you note was necessary since we brought our own bottle.

Thank-you notes are a way of life here, Beverly, and the whole business can be quite confusing. The first time I gave a party (in honor of someone I barely knew, for people I had never met), I received 15 handwritten thank-you notes within three days. The difficulty was that I couldn't figure out who they were from. They come in the form of a fold-over note-paper with only the initials of the correspondent, done up in a curly script at the top. Bag, Pot, Eel, Moo, all thanked me for a delightful, memorable and interesting evening. I hadn't a clue who was writing me. Of course, they signed their first names only. Even when I could decipher the signature, I still didn't know which Buffy, Muffy or Marge had written me.

Popsie came over to help.

"Who's Pot?" I asked. The signature was unreadable.

"Me, of course."

The writing on her letter was cramped and slantwise, running off the paper.

"It would have been legible if you typed it," I said.

Popsie shook her finger at me.

"First lesson, Sondra. No 'wife of' types a thank-you letter in Washington. All thank-you's must be handwritten. I sent it to you so you'll learn how to write one yourself. But don't expect any more because it's a waste of time sending thank-you notes to close friends. And for heaven's sake, don't send a thank-you note for a thank-you note. Unless someone sends you flowers to thank you for your party. Mind you, in that instance, a phone call is possible, if you know the unlisted number." However, Popsie added, "I'd put a subclause in that rule. If you receive thank-you flowers accompanied by a printed card from the Dredging Association of North America, no acknowledgment is needed."

"Should I be hurt if some people never send me thank-you notes?" I asked.

"No," said Popsie. "Those are usually Powerful Jobs like Melvin Thistle, Jr. from State and Lionel Portant, the World-Famous Columnist. They receive 70 invitations a week. Consider yourself lucky if they show up at your dinner. Mind you, Dexter and I have received separate thank-you notes from a Supremely Powerful Job and 'wife of,' both handwritten, for the same party. They are truly well bred and exceptions to the rule."

"Generally speaking," Popsie continued, "thank-you notes are a weathervane so far as a person's status is concerned. Once he loses his Powerful Job, 'wife of' will revert and write you notes saying she's grateful to be remembered. It's amazing," Popsie mused, "how attitudes change when the invitations drop from 70 a week to one every three months."

"Another rule to remember about thank-you notes," Popsie continued. "Never write them before you actually go to the party. Let me tell you what happened to Sonny Goldstone."

Beverly, I wrote you about Sonny, the Gilded Bachelor and Social Asset who connects Powerful Jobs with Profitable Jobs. He's invited to all the Best Parties on the Eastern Seaboard.

"Sonny," Popsie explained, "unlike most bachelors, is most punctilious about writing thank-you notes. Last year, his social life was so hectic the only way he could keep up with his thank-you notes was to write them before he actually attended the dinners and mail them on the same day. Well, there was rather a grand affair at the Metropolitan Club, black tie, in honor of a Supremely Profitable Job. Sonny wrote an especially fruity note ('loved the flower arrangements, wittiest toast I've heard in a donkey's year'). But something came up and he wasn't able to get to the party. He realized there was nothing for it except to call, make a joke out of the whole thing and ask the hostess to the Jockey Club for lunch. It was worse than he thought. Apparently, the host died the day of the party and the guests were turned away from the doors of the Metropolitan Club. Sonny was so desperate to get his hands on that thank-you note that he hung around all day in the Watergate lobby waiting for the mail to be delivered. It cost him $100 and three Chivas Regals, but Sonny intercepted his thank-you note between the lobby and the fifth floor."

"Do you have any more advice about thank-you notes?" I asked.

"Never mention the names of other guests. If you go out as much as I do, you'll forget whom you saw where. Avoid the specifics that might give you away."

"Should I keep the thank-you notes that people send me?"

"Only if their signature might be worth something when they're dead."

Now I have fold-over note-paper with my very own initials, SAG. But Beverly, I'll still be writing you on lined foolscap.

Your best friend,
Sondra

The Upper Media and Georgetown Chic

Dear Beverly,

I'm not surprised that you wonder why I keep mentioning Georgetown in my letters when I don't even live there. Georgetown is a district of Washington where you can walk your dog, peer into a candle-and-pillow shop and try and figure out where one house ends and the other begins. The average Georgetown dweller must have some money because even the brick row houses sell for a sum that Sonny Goldstone, the Gilded Bachelor, wouldn't deride.

But there is something about Georgetown that provokes a curl of derision on the lips, a tone of suspicion in the voice of many a Washingtonian who doesn't live there. At first I thought it was because the houses looked so inconspicuous and cost so much. It's not only that, Beverly. Georgetown has become kind of a myth for those who dwell within as well as out.

I've heard phrases like "Georgetown Elite," "Georgetown Snobbism," "Georgetown Has-Beens," and even "Georgetown Conspiracy." I've also heard of "Georgetown Chic" (although I must admit the last phrase is mostly used by those who dwell within). I'm not sure why this innocent-looking neighborhood arouses such strong feelings, Beverly, but I'm doing my best to find out.

I was lunching with "wife of" Thistle Jr. from State and her 8-year-old twins at Armand's Pizzeria (not far from her home in Cleveland Park) when she used the phrase "that Georgetown set."

"I take it," I said, "you're not a Georgetownophile?"

"Too much faded chintz and uninformed gossip," she said shortly, helping herself to the last wedge of deep-dish pizza.

I wondered if she was referring to the fact that Dexter Tribble is lobbying for her husband's job and had invited a few of the Upper Media (Lionel Portant and the likes) for dinner to leak Thistle Jr.'s problems.

About the chintz, Beverly. "Wife of" Thistle Jr. may have put her finger on something. When Popsie Tribble redecorated her Georgetown house she put down her $80-a-yard fabric in the sun for three weeks, "for maturation." It's the same method Thistle Jr.'s teenage daughter uses to fade her jeans.

Anyway, the next day I lunched with Popsie at the Jockey Club (not too many children eat there) and I repeated what "wife of" Thistle said.

"Sheer jealousy," Popsie sniffed. "Don't you know her background?"

"No," I said. "What is it?"

"She was actually born in Cleveland Park," Popsie replied.

Cleveland Park, Beverly, is a nice family neighborhood where a lot of young congressmen and senators live. You know the kind of place. No fences around the houses and perhaps a few too many purple azalea bushes.

Popsie continued.

"'Wife of' Thistle couldn't cope with a civilized dinner party even if she had the entire Protocol section of State helping her. Eat at the Thistles' in Cleveland Park and come to the Tribbles' for dinner in Georgetown. Then you'll see the difference. In Georgetown, we know how these things are done. I wouldn't live anywhere else. It's so cozy. And I can walk to all the parties, except when I have to fly to New York."

It's a queer thing, Beverly. Popsie talks about walking in Georgetown. I walk there all the time, but I never see Popsie strolling in front of her house. Or anyone else I know. Maybe Georgetown dwellers don't want to be confused with the tourists.

About a week after my conversation with Popsie, I sat beside Senator Pod at the Washington Hilton at the annual meeting of the Dermatologists Association of North America. The Senator had to be there because he was trying to corner the market on dermatologists' campaign funds in his state. We were there because of the word "North" in North America.

I asked the Senator what he thought about Georgetown.

"I don't think about it. It's Eastern Establishment. Who thinks about Eastern Establishment these days? No power there since the Kennedy period. The Democrats like Georgetown, except for Lyndon Johnson, of course. I agree with Johnson. It's a low-lying place and becomes dank in the summer. I call it Washington's Mosquito Belt."

"Do you ever go to Georgetown parties?" I asked.

The Senator changed his tone a little. "Sometimes I cross the moat," he said a little defensively.

"Why?" I asked.

"Because of the parlor-room access."

"Parlor-room access to whom?" I asked.

"To the Upper Media," the Senator replied. "It's more agreeable to set things right with the Upper Media over the fingerbowls. They still use those things in some houses in Georgetown. A few 'Used-to-be-Close-to's' and former Mr. Secretaries live there along with members of the Powerful Press. In Virginia they gossip about horses at dinner. In Georgetown, they gossip about politicians."

Beverly, I don't know if setting things right over the fingerbowls means that Senator Pod is leaking information. Or giving his version of the story, off the record, of course, to Lionel Portant. I just hope there are no listening devices in all those faded chintz settees.

Your best friend,

Sondra

Gift Atrocities

Dear Beverly,

I'm awfully worried about Christmas, and Popsie Tribble hasn't made things any easier. I don't know if you are aware of this, but for reasons hidden in the mists of protocol, Mr. Ambassador and "wife of" are supposed to send out gifts to Powerful Jobs and Close-Tos during the holiday season. Popsie was over the other day giving me the benefit of her advice.

"What gift atrocity are you sending out this year?" she asked. "I didn't think the choice you made last Christmas helped cement relations between our two countries."

Truthfully, Beverly, I was surprised. We gave away 100 beautifully bound books on insect behavior in the North-west Territories, with color photographs. But Popsie knows more about these things than I do, so I listened to what she had to say.

"At least it wasn't as bad as what Baron Spitte, the dusty diplomat, gave me."

"What did he send?"

"A paperback set of the real property laws of his country, written, I believe, in Turkish."

"But Baron Spitte isn't Turkish," I said.

"I think the Turks occupied his country until the 19th century. It must have been a re-issue of an old book."

I began to feel a bit defensive about this gift-giving business.

"Mr. Ambassador has received some gift atrocities too," I said. "When he went to Vermont for a day to give a speech, they presented him with a large block of green marble to take on the plane. He only had carry-on luggage with him so he had to hold the slab on his lap all the way to Washington.''

"What did Mr. Ambassador give to Vermont?'' Popsie asked.

"Place mats with maple leaves stamped on. At least they weighed less.''

"One has to be philosophical,'' Popsie said, "about this thing of countries, states or cities exchanging gifts. There is a perverse rule of thumb. The bulkiest gifts are always given to people taking off on planes. My Dexter, the Roving Ambassador, was always given boxed sets of folk dance records right on the tarmac, or bronze plaques with the mayor's face engraved on them. Once he was given a marble cheese board when he was going up in a seven-seater over the jungle in Central America.''

"Mr. Ambassador,'' I countered, "was handed a Lady Baltimore cake, eight layers of fig filling, and covered with tutti-frutti icing. He was returning from the Southwest and had to make three changes of planes.''

"What did he do with the cake?'' Popsie asked.

"He dumped it in the men's room at O'Hare.''

"There's no accounting for official gifts,'' Popsie said, "because they are decided upon by committees. A few countries, however, give nice presents. Except when that happens, Powerful Jobs like my Dexter have to hand over anything worth more than $165 to the Official Government Receptacle.''

Beverly, when I heard this phrase, I visualized a giant plastic garbage can stamped "U.S. Property.''

"The Official Government Receptacle,'' Popsie explained, "is in the Protocol Office at State. Eventually the General Services Administration auctions off the good stuff. I tried to give them all our folk dance records, but they took Sen. Pod's gold watch. It was presented to the senator by a certain Middle Eastern oil-rich country and had the coat of arms engraved on the back. Senators are occasionally reluctant to hand over the good gifts to the Official Government Receptacle, but Pod thought it was the better part of wisdom to do so given some bad publicity he had had that year. Anyway, auction time came around, and he thought he'd bid on his watch."

"What happened?" I asked.

"Well," Popsie replied, "the watch wasn't in the auction. The senator became suspicious. Had it been filched by a protocol officer? Pod thought there might be possibilities for a Senate investigation. The plot became thicker, however, when a clerk in the GSA told him *sotto voce* that the watch had actually been taken by someone in the FBI. The senator now believed he was on to something big and was ready to call a press conference. Much to his consternation, he had to cancel it when he found out the watch was worn as a prop by a burnoose-wearing FBI agent in the Abscam scandal. The watch eventually turned up at an auction and sold for $5,000."

"Who bought it?" I asked.

"Sonny Goldstone, of course."

"Well," I said, "Sonny likes nice things."

"For himself," Popsie said bitterly. "Do you know what he gave me for a Christmas present this year? Free Portuguese lessons and a white basketball. I made the mistake of telling him about my New Year's resolutions — that I would do more exercise and learn a new language."

"However," Popsie added with some satisfaction, "I'm not the only one who's been the victim of a gift atrocity. It's the Thistle Jr.'s anniversary this week and a big limousine drove up to their door. The chauffeur handed 'wife of' a beautifully wrapped box. The card on top said 'Happy Anniversary Melvin and Vera, with love from Joe and Dottie.'"

"Those are the Promisalls?" I asked.

"Indeed," Popsie replied, "Joe Promisall, the world's most expensive lobbyist."

"What was the gift?"

"An apparatus that holds nine boiled eggs, made of cut glass."

"Not too useful for picnics," I said.

"That's not the worst of it," Popsie exclaimed. "When 'wife of' Thistle dug down in the box she discovered another card saying 'Merry Christmas, Joe and Dottie, with love from Henry and Elsa.'"

"I don't understand," I said.

"They were given a floater-gift," Popsie explained. "That's the ultimate gift atrocity. You'll get it next year for Christmas from the Thistles."

Your best friend,

Sondra

The Washington Charity Ball

Dear Beverly,

You asked me what the holiday season was like in Washington. You're not the first. A reporter from *Time* magazine rang me up to ask if Washington parties were all that different from the eggnog and wassailing festivities that occur in Ottawa.

I thought of Popsie Tribble and her New Year's Eve dinner-dance this year. If you bother to read the foreign news, Beverly, you'll discover that the recently elected administration may or may not be making some important appointments. (I think we're going through something similar back home.) Three gentlemen-in-waiting are rumored to be in line for the same Powerful Job. Popsie wrote each of them a note saying, "If you are appointed, which I sincerely hope for the sake of our country, please come for dinner. If you are passed over, I would still like you to come, but afterward, for the dance."

A Washington hostess like Popsie Tribble never lets the holiday spirit interfere with her priorities.

Now there's another kind of festivity that occurs at Christmas as well as all year-around. The Washington Ball. As you well know, Beverly, I was never asked to any balls before I came here. I imagined a ball would be a gorgeous thing, like the second act of the Nutcracker Suite, where something wonderful happens, as it did to Clara, or Cinderella.

Popsie was the first to explain to me that balls in Washington are not quite like that.

"You're thinking of old-fashioned private balls with a snobbish and exclusive invitation list, paid for by the parents of Prince Charming. In Washington, we have charity balls, where a mere table costs at least $1,000. Only multinational corporations, senior partners of K Street law firms or successful lobbyists pay for balls in Washington. Not the King of Ruritania."

Popsie warned: "Sondra, don't wear your glass slippers at a charity ball because the CEOs are too tired and old to stoop and pick one up, even if you leave before the clock strikes 12 (which sensible people always do)."

Popsie continued with her advice: "If you go to a ball, always remove the centerpiece on the table, which some committee wife has labored for hours to contrive."

"That's not very nice," I said.

"If you don't," Popsie said, "you'll never see the people on the other side of the table. Not that you'll know who they are. If your host is a CEO, he'll choose his own guest list. There will be three colleagues from his company, for moral support, and an ambassador if the CEO thinks he's going to do business with that country."

"It doesn't sound very romantic," I said.

"Romance is for young people," Popsie said. "People who go to charity balls are well past 50. I hope you're not naive enough to think that you might be able to marry off an ugly daughter at a charity ball. Do your daughters have the clout to make a multinational corporation pay for their seats at the table?"

"Forget about the girls," I said. "At least I'll get to dance."

Popsie sighed. "Nobody will ask you except the oldest man there, who is usually a retired chairman of the board with lots of stock in the company. It's worth accepting because he's the only one who's had the time to freshen his fox trot. He's probably taking dancing lessons in Palm Beach."

Beverly, I wasn't going to give up on charity balls completely. "The conversation might be interesting," I said.

"No, it won't," Popsie said, "because there won't be any conversation. Just shouting. The band always plays too loud. All through dinner."

"If balls aren't for conversation or for young people," I asked Popsie, "what should I do with my grown-up unmarried children who are visiting me during the season?"

"Show them movies on your VCR," Popsie answered. "Everyone in this city is encumbered with elderly children coming home from college. Washington is a transient town. The children don't know each other."

"Maybe I should give an all-ages and all-stages party. You know, ask the parents with the children."

"Those things are never a success. The children hate them. Melvin Thistle's teen-age daughter will engage Mr. Ambassador in a long conversation so as to avoid talking to "son of" and "daughter of" Mr. Ambassador. "Son of" and "daughter of" will go upstairs to their rooms to avoid talking to Thistle's children. "Wife of" will find herself doing the same thing she does in Powertown all year long, except for one thing."

"What do you mean?" I asked.

"Instead of chatting up a Powerful Job," Popsie said, "you'll have to chat up his children."

Your best friend,
Sondra

Powertown's Post-New Year's Blues

Dear Beverly,

I haven't thanked you for your far-seeing gift, cruel though it was. How did you know that, come the first week of January, Mr. Ambassador and "wife of" would look like two bloodshot and bloated ghosts of Christmas past? Popsie Tribble, whose flesh has filled out as well, claims that the eye-level scale you sent comes in the category of gift-atrocity. But old friends like you and George are allowed to take liberties. I'll bring the scale in from the garage just as soon as I begin my steamed-fish-and-spring-water diet, which will be tomorrow, for sure.

Actually, I've noticed that a lot of people in Powertown are suffering some sort of remorse now that the holidays are over. Popsie says she's never going to give another New Year's Eve party. In the first place, the people she really wanted didn't show up, like Senator Pod, who is known for his misanthropic proclivities. He chose to spend the night alone in a cabin in Virginia with his Rhodesian Ridgeback. "Fleas are better than people on New Year's Eve," he told Popsie. (I don't know if I told you, Beverly, but the weather was so warm that the fleas were still hopping during the holiday season on Powertown's dogs.) But he sent along "wife of" Pod and his older brother to represent him. Brother Pod doesn't get out of Kazoo City all that often, so he really adored Popsie's party. He spent most of the time helping the waiters pop the Moet et Chandon. Popsie rang me the next day and said, "When I walked on my drawing room carpet" — 19th-century Chinese, Beverly — "I could feel the champagne squishing between my toes. How am I going to get body and house in shape for the Inauguration?" Popsie was close to tears.

To be fair, Beverly, Popsie put on a very good show on New Year's. It's the first time I've had more caviar than I could eat. Dexter Tribble, the Roving Ambassador, went to Moscow on a secret mission, and brought back six barrels of the fish eggs. I guess the customs people thought it was sauerkraut or something.

Now we're all a little sick of caviar. As old Baron Spitte, the Dusty Diplomat said, "I feel like a 40-year old pregnant sturgeon. Cut me open and you'll find me filled with the finest Beluga."

Lionel Portant, the World Famous Columnist and Media Star, is also rather gloomy. His New Year's predictions of who's in and who's out in the new administration were 100 percent inaccurate.

"Only the Used-to-be-Close-To's leak to me these days," he said mournfully, which I thought was a rather feeble excuse. He also made the mistake of answering his own phone during the holidays and committed himself to free speeches in Orlando, Tampa and Atlanta.

"My secretary knows I never give free speeches but she went on vacation. How do you fend off people who claim our our children sit together in the sixth grade, or say they knew me when I was a nobody and, since they still are nobodies, I haven't the right to let them down?"

Remember Sonny Goldstone, the Gilded Bachelor and Social Asset? Apparently some of his mergers have turned sour, "I'm going to move to Palm Springs," he told me, "and run the business from a coffee shop near my condo. There are too many people on my payroll. If I fire them, maybe I'll be able to recoup enough to buy a helicopter to take me to the dog races."

Despite Portant's prediction that Melvin Thistle, Jr. would be leaving State, Thistle is staying on. Remember how Popsie tried, with her little Georgetown dinner parties, to maneuver her Dexter into Thistle's job?

Well, Dexter is now in kind of limbo because Roving Ambassador jobs are being eliminated. The Bureau of the Budget believes this will help lower the deficit.

Beverly, it's getting close to the Inauguration and there are all sorts of parties that everyone is going to except Mr. Ambassador and "wife of" because we haven't been invited. "Wife of" Thistle says we should be glad because these parties are always very crowded and noisy and filled with Americans not from Washington. Nevertheless, she bought three dresses at a sale at Garfinckel's, which she hopes will suffice for all the events. Popsie's so depressed I'm afraid to ask her if she's been invited to the parties the Thistles have decided to attend.

It's colder now in Powertown, and the trees have a little frost on them. The vet says the day some ice forms on the ground I should suspend Sweet Pea in some kind of dip to get rid of the fleas. "More important," he added, "have your Residence fumigated precisely the moment your dog is being dipped, or the fleas will return."

The logistics, Beverly, are far too complicated for "wife of," and Mr. Ambassador says fumigation costs too much money anyhow. So I guess we'll forget about the whole business and scratch away during the Inauguration.

> *Your best friend,*
> **Sondra**

Inaugural Indignities—
The Podiatrist and
The President

Dear Beverly,

I suppose you want to know about the Inauguration. Since it was our first, we didn't know what to expect until a clue arrived in a form letter sent to us, not by the Protocol Department, but by someone more knowledgeable — a Washington podiatrist. In his letter he said that foot disorders during this period are particularly common among diplomats, senators and Mr. Secretaries, who spend much of their time at receptions and ceremonial events shifting their feet or, even worse, rocking back and forth on the heels instead of moving the feet forcefully from one place to another. (That latter phrase, I told Mr. Ambassador, tugging his arm at one of the Inaugural stand-up receptions, is a euphemism for going home to bed.) Joe Promisall, the world's most expensive lobbyist, also received the letter and, having a sharp eye for a bargain, thought we could get a group rate if we threw in Sen. Pod and Baron Spitte, the dusty diplomat, and Popsie Tribble, who attended every chic stand-up party during the Inaugural period.

"Maybe," Joe Promisall said, "we could even include the president." Promisall is something of a visionary, Beverly, which occasionally hampers his sense of reality.

I can't tell you about the parade because it was canceled on account of the cold weather. As usual the Powerful Jobs blamed Canada, so I told them if they intended to put quotas on our exports to the United States, our trade people would be ready to accept any limitation Congress desired on our wind chill factor and frigid air. Mr. Ambassador agreed that it would be a good bargaining chip.

Aside from the weather, bunions and heel spurs, there were two other aspects of the Inauguration festivities that disturbed "wife of": reading about the parties I wasn't invited to and reading about the parties I did attend.

At the parties I did attend I would usually spend my time talking to a familiar "wife of," amidst the maelstrom of people circling around us, about foot disorders and what the family did at Christmas. The next day I'd scan the social pages and discover I was at the same party as Don Rickles, Merv Griffin, Oscar de la Renta, a lot of the "W" set, and a fairly handsome actor who works on television named Tom Selleck. I didn't recognize any of them, Beverly, and, needless to say, none of them recognized me. Actually someone pointed out Tom Selleck, but I didn't approach him because I wasn't sure we had anything in common. The only conversation I have cultivated to any extent, since I've been in Washington, concerns trade imbalances. Somehow I didn't think he or even Don Rickles would go for that. Beverly, I did meet Esther Williams and told her I was a swimmer too. She responded politely but without the enthusiasm I had hoped for. I told Popsie that I wanted to try out trade imbalances on Frank Sinatra, but he wasn't at any of the parties I attended.

Popsie, of course, went to every "in" party. "Authentic 'in' party-goers," she explained, "like myself, become weary of hearing 'Hail to the Chief' played so often everywhere we go."

Popsie refused to attend the Inaugural balls.

"Once is enough. I don't want all those strangers from Wisconsin and Idaho pressing against my Herrera velvet."

Well, Popsie does know everybody who counts as well as how to behave at a large "in" party. She walks in with her eyes slightly unfocused, staring into mid-distance. This no-eye-contact technique prevents her from being trapped by former Mr. Secretaries, Used-to-be-Close-To's, as well as yours truly. She maneuvers herself beside a member of her peer group and whispers into the Famous Name's ear until she has to go to the next party.

Beverly, the technique works. Her name and picture appeared more often in the newspapers than any other "wife of" in Powertown. She has the clippings to prove it. And she's the first of our group to make an appointment with the podiatrist because of a potential hammertoe problem.

Mr. Ambassador went to the public swearing-in ceremony ("wives of" were canceled because of the weather) and told me everything went smoothly because the security had been organized by Kojak, who must have been hired especially for the event, since he was present at the Capitol during the ceremony.

We discovered that the Inaugural balls are not for dancing but for waiting. Over 40,000 people paid up to $125 a ticket to stand for hours until the band struck up the only tune they wanted to hear. Most people aren't "in" like Popsie, and waiting for "Hail to the Chief" didn't weary them at all.

The Inaugural is supposed to be over, Beverly, but a kind of half-life lingers on. The out-of-towners don't get out of Washington fast enough, so Popsie had to give a post-Inauguration cocktail for some Californians and New Yorkers. I wonder if anyone from Wisconsin has ever been in her house.

Your best friend,
Sondra

Laughter Nights in Washington

Dear Beverly,

Occasionally you ask a question that penetrates the squishy core of life in Powertown: "When do you people have any laughs?" Well, laughter exists in Washington but it's not as spontaneous as you and George might expect. The thing is, Beverly, you have to tell people beforehand, on an official invitation, that laughter is not only permitted at the event, but required. In this city nobody likes being taken unawares.

When we first came here, "wife of" didn't realize that there were publicly sanctioned Laughter Nights which are well-advertised beforehand so people know what to expect. Usually, official Laughter Nights are organized by the media and are supposed to relieve any little tensions that may have come up between the Powerful Press and Powerful Jobs.

The greatest expert on these Bacchanalia is Lionel Portant, the world famous columnist and media star, who deigned to give me a few tips on proper behavior at publicly sanctioned Laughter Nights.

1. Your goal is to endure the evening, not enjoy it.

2. Don't look happy. The correct expression on your face should be one of glum forebearance.

3. From time to time an indulgent smile is permitted, never raucous laughter.

4. Dozing in a sitting position is permitted. Sleeping on the hotel dining room floor can be controversial.

5. Eat fast and don't talk while dinner is being served so you won't slow up the service and prolong the evening.

6. Pray silently that they won't serve a separate course for the salad.

7. If someone says something particularly belittling about a Powerful Job, don't stare at him to see how he's taking it.

8. If someone says something genuinely funny, turn to your neighbor and tell him you know who actually wrote the speech.

9. Don't check your coat, unless you want to get home at daybreak.

A couple of years ago, Beverly, when Mr. Ambassador and "wife of" didn't know Washington very well, we tried to have some fun at a party and imported a famous comedian from Canada to entertain our guests. As soon as Mr. Ambassador announced the possibility of after-dinner laughter, whatever gaiety there might have been in the room ceased. A terrible silence gripped the company. Popsie Tribble actually left her place at one of the tables to tell me about my *faux pas*. (I don't think she was too thrilled where I sat her anyhow.)

"You never mentioned jokes on the invitation," she said reproachfully. "Don't you know that nobody laughs after 10 p.m. in Washington, unless there's an official warning?"

Popsie was right. As soon as we finished the maple-syrup mousse, Melvin Thistle, Jr. from State announced, "I'm expecting a call from Seoul" and left. Joe Promisall kissed me goodby, saying, "Love to stay and listen but I have to make a long-distance phone call to Baltimore."

Sonny Goldstone, the Social Asset and Gilded Bachelor, told me that he had to drive to Rockville because he had promised to sleep over at his mother's house.

The rest of them, Beverly, didn't even bother making excuses. Mr. Ambassador said I must have been hallucinating because of my hysteria, but I'm sure I saw Senator Pod trying to beat the crowd at the door by escaping through a window. Baron Spitte was the only one who remained, because he believes in standing by his colleagues, no matter what the indiscretion.

Never again, Beverly. Have you ever sat up all night with a depressed comedian trying to explain why there were only 10 instead of 100 in the audience? (The chef, the butler and four waiters truly enjoyed his performance.)

The next morning Popsie Tribble called me and said, "Sondra, don't ever bring in a foreigner if you really want to do something for laughs. We have our own publicly sanctioned funsters who will keep your guests riveted in their golden ballroom chairs."

"Who are they?" I asked.

"Art Buchwald, Senator Robert Dole and Former Chairman Robert Strauss."

"Are they expensive?" I wanted to know.

Popsie gave my question some thought.

"Two of them might come for free but not to promote Ontario rutabagas."

"Would live hogs from Gravelbourg, Saskatchewan, be more of a temptation?"

"You might be on to something there," Popsie said. "Why don't you give them a call?"

I'll tell you sometime, Beverly, what they said when I phoned them.

Your best friend,
Sondra

Senator Pod

Baron Spitte

Mr. Ambassador

Lionel Portant

Popsie Tribble

Melvin Thistle, Jr.

Sonny Goldstone

Wife of

Joe Promisall

6.
Powertown Players

Popsie Tribble and the Balance of Terror

Dear Beverly,

Too bad about your February blues, but you won't get rid of them by visiting me. It's the doldrums in Washington, too. Even Popsie Tribble is going through a mini-depression because all her friends were asked to go cruising down the Nile on a Famous Name's yacht and somehow she was left off the guest list. To compensate she's boning up on arms control, which is the "in" topic of conversation in Powertown.

Popsie attended a B-list party at Baron Spitte's ("He's getting old," she says, "and doesn't care.") where she met a Professor Otto Wither from Georgetown University who offered to give her arms control lessons in her home, for a fee. (He brings his own color slides and published articles.) Mr. Ambassador told me to join Popsie and be instructed because "wife of" knows only last year's topics — the election, which no one wants to hear about now, and the deleterious effect of Canadian pork imports on Nebraska's economy, which I never wanted to talk about even last year.

Before Popsie started her arms control lessons, she rang me up to tell me what a slump she was in.

"Do you know what I did this morning?" she said gloomily. "I'll give you a check list:

1. I wrote one thank-you note to the wife of Senator Pod who gave a hunger luncheon (day-old bread, processed

cheese slices and Washington water) to remember the starving. It cost me $50 and I didn't have a good time at all.

2. I put artificial tanning lotion on my face so now I look yellow instead of white.

3. Thought about having a pedicure, but who's going to see my feet in the next three months?

4. Made six phone calls to people who I know are here. Nobody answered except the maids. Everyone but me must be doing something interesting.

5. I tried to read an article about arms control in *The New York Review of Books* but put it down and picked up the *TV Guide* instead.

You notice, Beverly, it didn't sound like our old self-confident Popsie. But I think she started to perk up when Otto Wither began telling us about Mutually Assured Destruction and the Balance of Terror.

It was during our second lesson that Popsie had her idea.

"I'm going to give an Arms Control dinner, black-tie. Do you think I should make Merv the guest of honor," she asked the professor, "or will the other arms negotiators become jealous?"

Wither had dropped the name Merv amidst all those initials like GLCM, SLBM, INF, ASAT and ICBM.

"Merv," Wither explained a bit acidly, "is not an arms-control negotiator. Merv is not even a person. Merv means MIRV, which is a multiple independently targeted re-entry vehicle."

I'm sorry to say, Beverly, both Popsie and I looked blank.

"Perhaps I'm going too fast for you ladies," Wither said. "It's a missile, like all those other initials. But it can hold 10 atomic bombs, which can be fired separately, in different directions."

Popsie's always been very competitive, so I wasn't surprised when she asked, "Who has the most MIRVs?"

"The Russians," Wither said.

Popsie looked unhappy.

"Does that mean I have to leave Ambassador Dobrynin off my invitation list?"

"Not necessarily," "wife of" piped up, "the Americans have more SLBMs." I hoped that Wither would notice that I was smarter than Popsie.

But Popsie knew more than I guessed.

"Ice Station Zebra," Popsie said thoughtfully. "Rock Hudson was the captain of the nuclear submarine. Howard Hughes watched it over and over before he died."

Popsie suddenly had that smug look on her face which she gets when she knows she's going to conduct a social coup in Powertown.

"If I invited Kampelman, Glickman, Sen. Tower and Dobrynin to my dinner, that would create a strategic balance."

"Precisely," Wither agreed, "Think of Dobrynin as a MIRV and the American negotiators as SLBMs. You would definitely maintain the Balance of Terror at your party. Although," he said, "the Russians might insist that you invite a Karpov as well."

"What's a KARPOV?," I asked.

"Karpov is not a missile," Wither patiently explained. "He's a Soviet negotiator. Mrs. Tribble's dinner is certainly a social metaphor for Mutually Assured Destruction," Wither said happily.

Popsie was troubled. "I don't think I want that," she said.

"You don't understand," Wither explained. "Some experts believe Mutually Assured Destruction is a good thing. If the Russians MIRV us, we SLBM them. Both sides know that. So nobody does anything. It just means your party will not be destabilizing."

"Sounds dull, like one of Baron Spitte's dinners," Popsie mused. "Maybe I should have a Star Wars party."

"You mean you are going to ask an SDI for dinner?" I said, hoping I was using correct terminology.

"It would be worth destroying the Balance of Terror," Popsie said, "if everyone in town knew I had the President for dinner."

Your best friend,
Sondra

Joe Promisall, the World's Most Expensive Lobbyist

Dear Beverly,

When we were living the quiet life in Ottawa, I remember George pointing out a couple of ill-dressed fellows who were lounging about the lobbies of Parliament. He said they were five-percenters, who were trying to eke out a living introducing plumbing contractors to bottom-rank bureaucrats in Public Works. I believe George was toying with the idea of being a five-percenter, but you told me the sight of those losers drove him into the muffin shop business.

Well, Beverly, in Washington George would have chosen otherwise. Here five-percenters are called lobbyists and many of them wear $900 suits. Lobbyism is the growth ministry in Powertown, and Senators, Mr. Secretaries and even Ambassadors consider it a privilege to be seen in their company. Almost everyone who hasn't a government job dabbles in lobbyism, from housewives who take in part-time piecework, to super lawyers on K Street with six-figure incomes.

My first experience with a lobbyist occurred when I was not more than three weeks in Powertown. A nice-looking young man stood by my side for 20 minutes at a cocktail party and then made a date to take me to the Lincoln Memorial.

I told Popsie Tribble about my conquest, but she was not impressed.

"In Washington," she declared, "men do not linger with 'wives of' at cocktail parties, or take them on sightseeing tours. You are not young, Sondra, but you are inexperienced."

I thought Popsie was jealous, Beverly, so I added, "He also asked me to lunch at the Jockey Club."

"Don't get carried away," she replied. "Young men in this town do not spend money on women for the sake of their sparkling eyes, or whatever you think your charms might be. That fellow is a budding lobbyist. You are his conduit."

"A conduit to what?" I asked.

"A conduit to a contract. From your government. He thinks a good word from you might have some influence. Of course he's completely misguided."

Well, Beverly, I did have lunch at the Jockey Club with the young man, and Popsie was right again. His conversation disappointingly turned away from the subject of "wife of" and dwelt upon the formation of a constituency for frozen Canadian cod in Congressman Otterbach's state.

"Confidentially," he said, "an aide in the Congressman's office told me they were inundated by bags of mail from unhappy consumers who are longing for cheap frozen fish dinners."

I suppose it wasn't patriotic of me to feel a little let down, but I did learn a lesson. Now that I have become more sophisticated in the ways of Washington, the subject of lobbyism fascinates me.

Don't think that I disapprove of lobbyists. Life would be far less civilized in Washington without them. They throw agreeable parties, chat with "wife of" longer than most Mr. Secretaries, and don't mind telling the latest gossip, which is more than you can say about the Powerful Press, who have a tendency to hoard stuff for their columns and TV appearances.

Beverly, if you come here and want to meet Senator Pod, "wife of," and their Rhodesian Ridgeback, a lobbyist will be happy to provide access.

But I wasn't sure what they did other than those things, so I asked Joe Promisall, who is the world's most expensive lobbyist, how he spent his time.

Joe seemed glad to have a sympathetic companion. "Let's sit down," he said wearily. "I've just been to a congressional hearing on Marine Sanitation Devices. Nobody but a lobbyist would go to that. Have you heard about the Task Force on Uncontrollables?" I admitted ignorance.

"I'm not surprised. Nobody knows what it means except me and a couple of people in Congress. It's on my program for tomorrow."

"It was all so much simpler in the old days,' he sighed. "A round of golf and a case of booze for the Senator, and the bill was passed. Now I have to argue about manganese nodules with some puritanical staffer who has a PhD."

"How could you get a bill passed on a golf course?" I asked.

"Let's say," Joe explained, "I was representing soybeans. The Senator knew less about soybeans than I did. And his staffers were all relatives. On the ninth tee, I'd let drop that soybeans were nutritious and the Senator was so impressed he'd pass the bill."

"You mean a case of bourbon, a game of golf, and telling the Senator that soybeans are good for people doesn't work anymore?"

"I can barely remember the time when it did," Joe replied. "You know what's on my agenda this week? I have to talk about steel tonnage and throw-weights to Congressman Otterbach. In his office. But I won't let it clutter up my brain for more than half an hour."

"Why not?"

"I have to keep some room for encrypted telemetry."

Beverly, I was pretty impressed. "Why do you have to know about that?"

Joe shook his head. "Not sure. Maybe it has something to do with the Task Force on Telephone Configuration. It's possible that I err. But I don't think it could be related to the one on Government Efficiency and the District of Columbia. Say," he said, "how about going to that one instead of me?"

Your best friend,
Sondra

Social Triumphs of a Washington Hostess

Dear Beverly,

Well, the Great Destabilizer, Popsie Tribble, dropped over yesterday, and after 15 minutes conversation, I realized that you and I are mere corks upon the water. It's Popsie who's riding the wave.

"Wife of" hasn't spoken to Popsie for quite a time. I've been following Mr. Ambassador around in California, eating underdone duck breasts and warmed goat cheese salads. But that's not really the reason I haven't seen her. Popsie only likes to touch base every few months. As she explained when I first arrived, "In Powertown, it's best to keep your friendships casual."

I didn't know what she meant then but I think I do now. This is a town where status shifts so swiftly that a euphoric Powerful Job who never had time to return his phone calls can easily turn into a decompressing Used-to-be-Close-To whose telephone never rings. If the Tribbles become too friendly with an Important Job who loses his power, it's awkward for Popsie to explain to the "wife of" why she dropped them from her party list.

When she did come over, Popsie certainly looked tip-top in her fawn leather pant suit. "I'm going through my renaissance period," she said happily. "I bought this in Milan, size 6."

"You look like Tina Turner," I said. "Did it cost a lot?"

"Not as much," Popsie said, "as buying the property next door to us in Georgetown and making it into tennis courts, which will help Dexter in his new job."

Beverly, I didn't know Dexter had a new job. I assumed that it must be far more lucrative than being a Roving Ambassador.

"Has Dexter left the government?" I asked.

"Not at all," Popsie said. "It's still a secret but he's going to be a Special Assistant in the White House. There's even talk of installing a bathroom in his office, which is next door to You-Know-Who."

I was mystified, and asked, "You mean he's had such an upgrade in salary that it will pay for the tennis courts?"

"Certainly not," Popsie said. "But now Dexter can play with the vice president, and all the media stars want to book a court on Saturday afternoon. Our courts will be the foremost source of leaks in Washington. Too bad you and Mr. Ambassador don't play tennis. You know what they say: 'No tennis. No access.'"

I was downcast. It would have been nice for Mr. Ambassador to start his telegrams with, "While I was playing singles with the vice president, I learned that..."

But I still couldn't figure out about the money. "How are you going to pay for all this?"

"From the advance I've received on my book," Popsie answered.

"What book?" I asked. "You've never written anything in your life except a thank-you note."

"It's called 'Partying to Win,' and it's subtitled, 'Social Triumphs of a Washington Hostess.' I hope they don't start video taping before the courts are finished."

"Why not 'How to Win New Friends and Drop Old Ones'?" I asked.

"Now don't be sour," Popsie chided.

"How much have you written?"

"I don't have to write it," Popsie explained. "All I do is talk into a tape recorder. Some editor will figure out about the paragraphing and things like that."

Beverly, you know that I've done some professional writing, so I was a bit dashed, especially when she said, "Actually, the video tapes are more important than the book. My agent believes they'll reach a larger audience than Jane Fonda's exercise tapes. All those Yuppies out there want to know how to fold a napkin."

"You don't know how to fold a napkin," I said. "Your housekeeper does it."

"That's why they gave me such a large advance," Popsie explained. "I have to give her a cut. But only on the book rights."

"Even if you haven't written the book, you must have some kind of outline in your head," I said.

Popsie thought a bit. "I've a couple of chapter headings. How about 'What to Serve at Après Tennis Off-the-Record Conversations'?"

"Double vodkas, I assume..."

"In the middle of the afternoon?" Popsie replied. "You still don't know much about Washington, Sondra. Iced tea or light beer are the only permissible beverages. Powerful Press and Powerful Jobs never get drunk with each other before the sun goes down."

"Do you have any other ideas for your book?" I asked.

"How to cope with ambassadors' wives."

"What do you mean, cope?"

"They're always asking you to boring fashion shows, luncheons, documentary film showings about their countries. A 'wife of' a White House person should never play favorites. It's best to avoid 'wives of' ambassadors completely, except if they give a lunch in honor of me."

"You mean you'll never come to the embassy unless I give a party in your honor?"

"You're different," Popsie said. "I've known you such a long time that you come into the classification of an old friend."

Beverly, I was not sure this was one of Popsie's High Priority categories.

"Just let me see your guest list beforehand," she continued. "If you're inviting someone more important than Dexter, we'll do our best to come."

"What do you mean, 'do your best'?"

"Try to be flexible," Popsie said soothingly. "Allow me the privilege of choosing my dinner partner. You know what I mean: someone who might be helpful to Dexter or a Famous Name, so they can take pictures of me with him for W."

Beverly, I suppose Popsie will always be asked to my parties. But I just might switch her place card at the last minute and sit her next to that dusty diplomat, Baron Spitte.

Your best friend,
Sondra

Golden Hands and the Jell-o Collector

Dear Beverly,

I wish you'd stop asking me about "Star Wars," Nicaragua and the latest front-line news about our frozen TV-dinners war with the United States. I've spent the last while in a D.C. hospital having what is called major but hum-drum surgery, and "wife of's" mind has become fixed upon herself. (Not that my doctor's actual work was hum-drum; Baron Spitte assured me he had the Golden Hands.)

By now you realize I'm going to bore you with hospital stories. What else does a convalescent have to brood about? Everyone says that medical science has made a lot of progress since we had our babies, but as far as I'm concerned, the nursing profession has taken one giant step backward, especially for paranoid patients like me.

Beverly, where have all the uniforms gone? A doped-up post-operative whiner needs the reassurance of nurses in formal attire. I mean caps, white stockings, even flying capes and a graduate medal pinned to a crisp authoritative uniform. Look, I'd even settle for a mere two stripes on the nonexistent cap, which used to denote two years of training.

This new dress-as-you-please nurse can really be confusing. Let me give you an example.

The day after my operation as I lay fetus-like against the side bar on my bed, a girl wearing a plaid shirt and corduroy trousers walked in and announced, "Let's have a look at that incision."

Beverly, she seemed pretty suspicious, and I said, cannily, "I thought people who worked downstairs in the canteen weren't supposed to inspect incisions."

She ignored me, thinking it was the morphia talking, and had her way.

I concluded that this must be how the head honcho nurse dressed. When another girl similarly garbed came into my room an hour later I decided to take her into my confidence.

"I think I'm going to be sick."

She jumped back to the doorway and said, "Honey, I don't do anything here except collect the Jell-o the patients never eat," and then disappeared, leaving my Jell-o.

Well, you understand my confusion. A paranoid patient needs to be able to tell the difference between those who offer painkillers and those who occasionally empty the waste basket. I'm old-fashioned, Beverly, and believe the Middle Ages had some good ideas we ought to copy now.

In those days, you knew precisely who you were dealing with. The king always wore his crown, the peasant his smock, the fishmongers and goldsmiths wore the distinguishing Guild livery, and tailors wore their tailoring caps, or whatever.

Now, wouldn't life be simpler if everyone in Washington wore something that told you what they did? Lobbyists could wear knee breeches, like courtiers. Present Mr. Secretaries might choose a nice lightweight polyester robe of office to differentiate themselves from former Mr. Secretaries. And of course, the media definitely need identification. I think Lionel Portant would be pleased to wear a medallion in the shape of a word-processor dangling from a ribbon around his neck. Republican and Democratic congressmen could wear cotton donkey and elephant hats, respectively. The senators would need hats with ampler ears, befitting their status. Mr. Ambassador, of course, would have to go back to donning the cocked hat with plume, but just to make sure he's not mistaken for an ambassador from another country, maybe he should wear a hockey helmet under the plume.

Anyhow, Beverly, back to the hospital. Things became better when I got out of bed and I learned to hang around the nurses' station. I never could get the knack of disentangling the I.V. tube patients shuffle around with, and someone at the station would usually unwind me, sometimes the secretary.

Baron Spitte, the gentleman, sent me yellow roses, but one of the girls (R.N.? nursing assistant? Jell-o collector?) told me the hospital had no vases. It was Golden Hands who couldn't stand the sight of the wilting flowers and carefully arranged them in a clean urine receptacle.

Beverly, aside from Golden Hands, the only persons in the hospital who were a cinch to identify were the Golden Hands-To-Be. Here are their characteristics:

1. They come in pairs.

2. They wear white coats, sort of protective covering, I guess, to make them look older.

3. They lack the authoritative manner of the Jell-o collector, and in fact, are the only persons on the ward who look more nervous than the patients.

4. Only one of them talks. "Hello, I'm Dr. Green and this is Dr. Blue. We'd like to do a little palpitating."

I realized, Beverly, this was the sole time during my stay in the hospital that I had any bargaining chips. I was pretty sure that the speechless one wasn't really a doctor.

"If you two are going to cause me any more pain, there are some things you must do first," I said. "Get me my ice water, which has been sitting on that bureau out of my reach for many hours."

Dr. Green, the older one, nodded to the speechless Dr. Blue. "Get her some fresh stuff from the ice water room."

"When you're out there, I added, "bring me some towels, a fresh nightgown, and while we're waiting, Dr. Green here can straighten out the lumps in my bed."

Beverly, they did everything I asked. I was wondering if they'd go as far as giving me a massage. (Massages have gone the same way as the nurses uniforms.) But I refrained from asking. As the song says, about poker and life: "You have to know when to play them..."

Your best friend,
Sondra

The Quail Breast and Crayfish Circuit

Dear Beverly,

Baron Spitte, the dusty diplomat, told me that one of the greatest hazards of his trade is coping with the gastronomic oddities of diverse nations. Naturally, you wouldn't think "wife of" would have anything to worry about in the United States. I was pretty certain no one would offer us the eye of a sheep because we were honored guests at a formal banquet in Pasadena. Although when we first came to Washington, Popsie Tribble warned us, "There's a downside to everything. Mr. Ambassador will have to talk about Canada to businessmen in hotel dining rooms across the country. Which means you'll be on the rubber-chicken circuit."

Oh, Beverly, would that it were true. The Holiday Inns, Hiltons, Marriotts, Sheratons and Westins have become born-again hotels. No more chicken and mashed potatoes, no more Irish stew. Mr. Ambassador and "wife of" have just returned from the western region of this country, and we're up to here in underdone duck breasts and buffalo cheese pizzas.

Beverly, the tribal customs are ferocious.

Let me describe one of our experiences in a remote region of California. It was the fifth day of our journey, and the local chief and some of the elders asked us to a banquet at one of the native restaurants.

"I recommend," the chief said, "rabbit filet and veal liver with honey and caraway sauce. And how about warm duck salad for a starter?"

Beverly, "wife of's" stomach was churning. He noticed my diplomatic silence and tried to be helpful: "My wife usually has duck consommé, followed by veal with crayfish."

Now, you might think the latter offering would be acceptable, Beverly, but believe it or not, Mr. Ambassador and "wife of" had eaten something made from duck and veal and crayfish every day of our California trip.

"May I have a small steak?" I whispered.

The chief was horrified. "You want red meat? Nobody in this part of California eats red meat."

Not only did I break a tribal taboo, Beverly, I learned something about official eating while traveling as "wife of." Whatever obscure regional dish I ordered of my own free will the first day inexorably turned up as the only choice on the menu for the rest of my stay. Red fish smothered with pecans in New Orleans, quail breasts with crayfish in Texas and, on a previous trip to California, tepid duck breasts served with blackberry butter and crayfish.

I also have become so obsessed with slow service at large dinners, Beverly, that you may have been right in your last letter when you said, "Sondra, it's time for you to come home."

At a banquet in New York, we waited one hour for the mesquite-grilled lamb chops and only had sweet white wine to tide us over. In Atlanta, there was a 48-minute lapse between dessert and the first speech. (Remember my bad back, Beverly.) In Washington, Senator Pod's wife, notorious in this town for being a slow feeder, held up the service at our table by eating the enoki mushrooms in her spinach salad one by one. I wanted to slap her.

"Wife of" has become so crazed with the desire for quick service that Popsie Tribble told me a deal of bad will was created between the two countries at our last dinner. We had a party in honor of the 12th most Powerful Job in Washington (that particular week), and I was determined that each course was only going to last eight minutes.

My butler had a stopwatch, there were more waiters than guests, and the meal was supposed to be finished by 9:45, including toasts. Beverly, when we sat down, a third of the guests hadn't arrived.

But wouldn't you know my luck. The chef banged out some rather good high-cholesterol food. In Washington, the rule is people care more about where they sit than what they eat. But that night, the Close-To's, Used-to-be-Close-To's, Powerful Jobs and all "wives of" thought they were at some Chaine de Rotisserie Gourmet feast and wanted to linger over their food. When the waiters removed the New Brunswick caviar before some of the guests were quite finished, I heard a muttering in the room. A waiter had to speak sharply to Dexter Tribble because he refused to let go of his plate.

During the main course (filet mignon with fresh *foie gras*), I signaled for removal at the eight-minute interval. Joe Promisall grimly held on to his wine glass and Sonny Goldstone actually threw his body over his plate. Mr. Ambassador yelled at me from his table, "For heaven's sake, let them finish eating."

But, Beverly, I was like a mad woman, and at dessert time (spun sugar covering sort of a frozen eggnog) the guests only had time to crack the carmel when the waiters attacked again. A lot of plate-tugging went on, and Popsie Tribble, who never takes dessert, perversely held down her dish with one hand and ate very slowly with the other.

I've got to get over this morbid affliction, Beverly, or Mr. Ambassador says we'll be forced to leave. He's even thinking of making me stay upstairs when we have dinner parties.

Your best friend,
Sondra

The Fast Lane

Dear Beverly,

So you're not sure that opening a second muffin shop means that you and George will finally experience life in the fast lane. (By the way, congrats for achieving street level this time; Mr. Ambassador believes it's a better location than the mall basement if you want to target that upscale market.)

You mentioned "traveling in the fast lane" before, and the expression makes me ponder. It's a popular phrase, but in Powertown at least, I don't think it means being a dope fiend. Actually, Beverly, I'm not sure what people are trying to say when they use the phrase here. Does it mean that people who move in the Fast Lane hobnob with famous names? I decided to ask Popsie Tribble, Washington Hostess and Socialite, what she thought. Her version goes something like this:

1. Traveling in the Fast Lane means you can get any Powerful Job to come to your party, even at the last minute. The seven other invitations that Powerful Job has put on hold will be regretted immediately.

2. Fast-Lane People never have to introduce themselves, or be the first to say hello, or even move at a party. They are always at the center of the densest part because others come to them (unlike "wife of" Mr. Ambassador who usually circles outside the mass, close to the walls, staring at people's shoes).

3. People who live in the Fast Lane buy their clothes at cost at Oscar's, Bill's or Mollie's.

4. If you're a Fast-Lane Woman, you will be placed beside the most Powerful Job because the hostess thinks

Powerful Job will be flattered. And if you seem a tiny bit bored, Powerful Job will instantly stop talking shop.

5. Fast-Lane Women don't have to wear Important Stones. But the "right people" will know she owns them.

I asked Popsie if she considered herself to be a Fast-Laner. Popsie reflected. "Yes, when I want to be. But my Dexter" — he's the White House Aide — "needs his quiet time now and then."

Well, Beverly, I wasn't satisfied that a Washington Hostess (even Popsie Tribble) knows everything about the Fast Lane. There must be something more to it than how you're treated at parties. So I went to Sonny Goldstone, the Gilded Bachelor, and asked him.

His version was a little different from Popsie's.

1. Nobody travels in the Fast Lane unless his annual income exceeds $1 million.

2. Movie actresses and European royalty (either sex) want to be seen in the company of Fast-Laners.

3. The maitre d' keeps a table for you whether you come or not. It must be the right restaurant, though.

4. Fast-Lane People know the current unlisted numbers of other Fast-Laners, who like to change them every month.

5. Fast-Lane People own their planes (or know how to get lifts with those who do).

6. The media should mention you frequently and favorably.

"And," he added, "Popsie Tribble does not travel in the Fast Lane."

I was a little offended by Sonny's last comment, for Popsie's sake, so I asked Sonny if he was a Fast-Laner. Sonny winked at me and said: "The secret of life in the Fast Lane is making other people believe you're in it."

Beverly, I was pretty confused. Sonny concentrates more on money than Popsie. But Popsie does get her picture in *Women's Wear Daily*. Maybe Sonny's in *Fortune*.

Anyhow, I bumped into Melvin Thistle, Jr. from State — he gets his picture in all the papers — and asked what living in the Fast Lane meant to him. He made these points.

1. Money doesn't count. Power counts.

2. Access and more access to the Supreme Commander.

3. Everyone returns your phone calls. When you return theirs, at 6 a.m., they're so flattered they forget what favor they wanted. (Merely grateful to hear your voice.)

4. Telling Cary, Burt, Meryl and Barbara about world affairs at a State Dinner and never being interrupted.

When I repeated what Sonny and Popsie had said, Thistle Jr. added: "Traveling in the Fast Lane doesn't mean being the center of attention only at parties in New York and Washington. You have to include Dallas and Los Angeles. Nobody has heard of Sonny Goldstone in Dallas or Los Angeles."

Beverly, I still felt there was something lacking in all the explanations. Maybe it's because I spoke to people who all believed they traveled in the Fast Lane.

Now, Baron Spitte, the Dusty Diplomat, is not a Fast-Laner. But he's been around Washington a long time and has observed a few things in Dallas and Palm Springs, where he attends those galas and balls.

He was having his afternoon nap at the Residence when I dropped by. But the Baron didn't mind being wakened because he was interested in the subject.

Baron Spitte, being the old-fashioned kind of diplomat, enjoys a metaphor. His answer went like this:

"Dear lady, the trouble with traveling in the Fast Lane is worrying that you won't stay in it. Especially in Washington, where nobody travels in the Fast Lane for very long. You know in New York and California they have very interesting landscapes with amusing side roads to follow and pleasant valleys that hide the Fast Lane from view. I'm afraid that in Washington, all valleys and side roads are connected to the Fast Lane. And the Fast Lane is Power. Some Powerful Jobs believe they'll fall into one of those big black holes on the side of the highway if they ever get off the Fast Lane. But here nobody has power forever," the Baron concluded, "except perhaps" — sighing as he sipped his iced tea — "the Press."

Beverly, I don't know if there are telephones in these big black holes on either side of the Fast Lane. But I do know one thing. No one in Powertown likes to be disconnected.

Your best friend,
Sondra

7.
More Perils
of Powertown

Mr. Rochester's Mad Wife and Embassy Party Life

Dear Beverly,

You're not the only one who's asked me if I "get sick and tired of giving those embassy parties." I'm a little sensitive about the question because it could imply that "wife of" has a frivolous nature, while you and the others have loftier goals in life. Be that as it may, parties are my business. And as wife of Mr. Ambassador, I've made a detailed study of the kinds of parties we have given.

1) *The Breakfast Party.*

Which is never called a party by Mr. Ambassador. They are meetings or briefings to which "wives of" are never asked. You'd think I'd be off the hook, Beverly, but these early-morning gatherings still present a problem. I'm locked in upstairs, like Mr. Rochester's mad wife, trailing around the bedroom in her nightgown, wondering if she should set fire to something so the guests will leave a little sooner. There is one consolation. Mr. Ambassador always comes upstairs with his usual report, "The rolls were stale." and then leaves with the guests.

2) *The Mid-Morning Coffee Party.*

Only for "wives of" who represent different charitable organizations including Congress. For some reason, they like to gather in an embassy to discuss their projects. There is always a male who gives a pep talk about the forgotten art gallery, the forgotten disease, the forgotten people, while "wives of" munch on carrot cake.

3) *Working Luncheon.*

Mostly a repetition of the breakfast meeting, but with fresh rolls and a different cast of characters. "Wife of" should get out of the house or is again locked in upstairs. "Wife of's" only duty is to make up the menu.

3a) *Ladies' Luncheon.*

Everything must look exceptionally attractive, including the food, which nobody eats. Daiquiris may be served, but are never finished. Some tension between "wives of" who have to go back to the office and those who don't.

3b) *Visiting Artist's Luncheon.*

When a famous Canadian writer (Farley Mowat?) or cultural figure comes to Washington, it is Mr. Ambassador's duty to promote his career by giving a lunch. "Wife of" is present. Powerful Jobs are never asked because they are interested in politics, not culture. These luncheons can be disastrous if book reviewers and critics send in lowly proxies who have never heard of the artist and announce the fact as they come in. A successful artist's luncheon includes genuine admirers, bookstore owners and members of the arts community in Washington who accept because they want to see an embassy. Guests at artist's lunches, unlike those at working or ladies' lunches, will always take a cognac or two as a digestif. "Wife of" has only one problem with artist's luncheons. It's hard to know what to do with the guests at 4 o'clock in the afternoon.

4) *Full Silver Service Tea Party.* (at which coffee must be served)

Similar to the mid-morning coffee parties because the guests are all women who have something to do with a charity. The ladies talk in whispers and like the chocolate truffle best.

4a) This sub-category tea party is for tourists who come in buses for a half-hour stop. The bus group are usually widows on art gallery tours, a few widowers and their leader, a male curator. They stay only half an hour because the bus is expensive and waiting to take them back to the hotel. The group, which has already visited every museum in Washington, shows signs of dehydration and exhaustion. Members look longingly at our swimming pool rather than our pictures and sometimes put their feet in our little splashing fountain.

5) *The Cocktail Party* (cold canapés only).

Sub-categories: Cocktail Reception (hot food on sticks), Cocktail Buffet (hot food on table).

This is the most dangerous kind of party for an embassy to give because the invited do not think it's necessary to say whether they are actually coming or not. There are either too many (guests bring relatives, etc.), or nobody comes at all.

The most trying cocktail reception "wife of" ever experienced occurred when we decided to tantalize Americans with the idea of holding their conventions in Canada. I was told by our Tourist Section that if we gave a decent party for the convention organizers ("be nice to the ones with the blue name-cards"), Toronto would stand to make a bundle instead of Atlantic City. Well, Beverly, 300 people came, and I must say it was a mixed group. Members of associations representing the Psychiatrists, Beauticians, Tree Surgeons, Trial Lawyers, Meat Packers and Gasoline Retailers of America stood about, wondering who everyone else was. The Psychiatrists were the most well-behaved, tiptoeing around looking at our pictures. The Tree Surgeons and Beauticians hit it off and made plans to go out to dinner together after the cocktail party. Unfortunately, the Meat Packers and Gasoline Retailers just began to enjoy themselves when "wife of" thought the party was supposed to be over. They took off their ties and moved the furniture so they could sit down and be comfortable.

"Close the bar," my social secretary said, "and they'll understand it's time to go." That wasn't such a good idea,

Beverly, because they just lifted off the bottles from the trays as the waiters disappeared into the kitchen.

"Turn off the lights," she said.

Gasoline Retailers and Meat Packers don't mind whether lights are left on or off. Mr. Ambassador and "wife of" left them at the Residence and went out to dinner with the Tree Surgeons and Beauticians. I still haven't had a report from our Tourist Section if any of these groups ever held a convention in Toronto.

Number 6, Beverly, is the dinner party, about which I have written you many times before. It is a subject fraught with so many categories, and ensuing anxieties, that not even a whole letter would do justice to the perils that lie within it. Dinner parties are thesis material, and the only one I know who merits a PhD in the subject is Popsie Tribble.

Your best friend,
Sondra

The Real
Senator Pod

Dear Beverly,

When I first came here I didn't know anything about the Senate, its members or its power. Popsie Tribble doesn't mix much with those on the Hill, but she gave me some pointers notwithstanding.

1) The Senate is part of Congress.

2) You can't get a Scotch Mist in the Senate Dining Room, but you can get your photograph taken.

3) Senators always come late, if at all, to dinner. "And," she added, "don't feel hurt if they won't come to your embassy. When did the Canadian government last contribute to their campaigns? And let's face it," she said, lighting her Balkan Sobranie, "Mr. Ambassador needs them more than they need him. You don't vote so you can't deal. Which means your country is zero on a senator's priority list. It would be best for his ego if Mr. Ambassador avoided the Senate completely."

Despite Popsie's advice, he does make his visits to the Hill. It's not all that bad waiting in the anteroom of a senator's office, because Mr. Ambassador gets to meet so many different kinds of people. (The Senate staffers have a tendency to overbook, like the airlines.) Waiting with him are Boy Scouts, mothers of fund-raisers, office seekers, mostly from the home state, and Joe Promisall, the lobbyist or one of his proxies.

Sometimes there are young people with sleeping bags who look as if they might spend the night. Mr. Ambassador doesn't mind waiting (senators are never on time, even on their home turf) because the female staffers are usually good-looking. He often wonders if the senator picks them personally.

Beverly, senators must be careful about their public image because they have to get elected every six years, something like the president of France. A local magazine recently sent a questionnaire to all the senators asking them details about their private lives. Popsie thinks some of them were a little overcautious in their answers, which, in her opinion, would make them appeal only to the wimp vote in their respective states.

Senator Pod came out as a real Caspar Milquetoast. This is puzzling because he told me himself there were no wimps in his constituency.

Popsie has her own view of Senator Pod, which differs from the magazine's. Let me describe how the Senator, or his staffer, or possibly "wife of," dealt with the questions and than what Popsie says.

Bad Habits (Magazine)
Eats chocolate. Has holes in his socks. Is consistently early for appointments.

Bad Habits (Popsie Tribble)
Only talks about himself. (I presume Popsie once sat beside him at dinner.) Is consistently late.

Favorite drink (Magazine)
Orange juice. There's an especially good orange juice made by a factory in his home state that the senator always keeps on hand.

Favorite drink (Popsie Tribble)
Likes martinis straight up in a five-finger tumbler.

Style of Dress (Magazine)
Conservative but casual. Buys all his clothes from a little haberdasher in his home state.

Style of Dress (Popsie Tribble)
She saw him buying a yellow cashmere coat in that men's store on Fifth Avenue in New York where you have to make an appointment to get in.

Hero (Magazine)
Giuseppe Delano Norseman. (You and I and Popsie don't know this person. But "wife of" guesses he must be a famous historical figure among some ethnic group in his home state, who always votes Democratic.)
Hero (Popsie Tribble)
Sounds right.
Favorite Vacation Spot (Magazine)
Famous river in home State.
Favorite Vacation Spot (Popsie Tribble)
She saw him tanning naked on Mustique, an island in the Grenadines.
Aspirations After the Senate (Magazine)
Savoring life by a famous river in his home state.
Aspirations (Popsie Tribble)
Say he's negotiating right now with Sonny Goldstone, the Gilded Bachelor and Social Asset. Looking for a five-figure income *après*-Senate.
Closest Friend (Magazine)
"Wife of" Pod and his Rhodesian Ridgeback.
Closest Friend (Popsie)
Pretty staffer in his office.
Spouse's Job Interest (Magazine)
Runs a nonprofit organization for indigent lumbermen (lumber is big in his home state) and writes a chatty news-letter to constituents.
Spouse's Job Interest (Popsie)
Hard to say. She hasn't been seen in public for the last three years. Maybe he killed her.
Favorite Food (Magazine)
McDonald's hamburgers.
Favorite Food (Popsie)
Loves fresh Russian caviar. When her Dexter was Roving Ambassador, Senator Pod always asked him to bring back a kilo or two. Pod usually confirms Dexter's jobs in the administration.

Favorite Books (Magazine)

Anything of an uplifting nature. The Bible and biographies of Lincoln, Churchill and Roosevelt.

Favorite Books (Popsie)

She saw him buying Penthouse in People's Drug Store on Dupont Circle. (I can't believe this, Beverly, because Popsie never goes to drug stores. I think she's just being spiteful.)

We'll never know which is the real Senator Pod, Beverly — the wishy-washy version in the magazine or Popsie's description. One thing is clear. Popsie's keeping a secret file in case he runs for president.

Your best friend,
Sondra

With Cooking Comes Power

Dear Beverly,

I realize you think "wife of" sounds spoiled when she complains about the chef. Especially since you and George are up to your elbows in muffin batter (or is it bagel dough now?) five days a week. Now be fair. You know how I used to like to cook. Staring in other people's fridges was my favourite recreation during Ottawa years. Well there are four fridges in the kitchen here, but the chef hates it when I enter his domain. So now I hardly ever enter the kitchen and you'd be surprised at the problems that can arise.

Last week we were having some international bankers for dinner, and I told Phillipe, our chef, who only speaks French, that roast beef was safest for that group.

But Phillipe wanted to serve a Washington specialty.

"What's a Washington specialty?" I asked.

"Ligeter," he said firmly.

Well, Beverly, he's only been here a short while and I was surprised he knew more about Washington than I did. I did mention Ligeter to Popsie Tribble. "It must be French for crab cakes," she said.

"I don't think French for crab cakes is Ligeter," I replied. But Popsie insisted on looking it up in the Larousse Gastronomique. She couldn't find Ligeter anywhere but she did discover that the French word for crab is crabe. I knew that already Beverly, but you know that you don't tell Popsie anything.

"Do you know what Ligeter looks like?" Popsie asked.

I didn't, although I searched for it. I went down to my forbidden kitchen at midnight and actually opened some of the fridge doors. All I could see were a bunch of leftovers, some Canadian fiddlehead ferns, and maple syrup that I'm trying to convince Phillipe to use.

I knew I had to clear up this business with Phillipe the next day. We had a face-off in the middle of the kitchen.

"Ligeter," I said. "What's Ligeter in English?"

"Some word, Madame, French and English." Phillipe was getting the hang of the language.

"Draw me a picture," I insisted.

He drew an animal with a long tail and big teeth.

"Alligator. Washington specialty," he pronounced.

You see, Beverly, the problems that can arise when someone else does the cooking for you.

Another thing, you know how I like to serve our national specialties, like fiddleheads and maple syrup, to our American guests.

We even tried Alberta buffalo meat which was not a success but I discovered a vodka from Alberta which we serve with New Brunswick and Manitoba caviar. The butler is in charge of the booze, Beverly, and I thought all was well in that area at least. After a year and a half I asked our lady-butler if we needed to reorder our much admired Alberta vodka.

"It's not necessary, Madame," she said, and showed me three empty bottles of the Alberta stuff.

"We just take the Smirnoff," she said, "and pour it into the bottles. Nobody knows the difference."

I know you envy me Beverly. As you say, it must be marvelous to have a French chef who can cook everything from sweetbreads Normande to alligator. But a peculiar phenomenon has come over Mr. Ambassador. He's been waking up in the middle of the night, moaning for strange foods.

Our nocturnal conversations go like this.

"Let's order a pizza," he says. "I saw an ad in the newspaper about a place in Spout Run that's open 24 hours, and they deliver." "Don't be silly," I answered. "You just ate *lapin au vin rouge* for dinner."

"I hate rabbit," he replied. "I left it on my plate. Can we have spareribs tomorrow? He never makes spareribs." (Mr. Ambassador always refers to the chef as he.)

"Spareribs are fattening," I said reproachfully. "I don't think embassies are supposed to serve spareribs at fancy dinner parties."

"Is that what Popsie Tribble says?" Mr. Ambassador sounded sarcastic. "How about hamburgers or hot dogs? I would really love a good hot dog. It's hard to remember what a hot dog tastes like," he said wistfully.

"Let's go to the movies tomorrow, at least we can buy some popcorn there, without butter of course."

"You forget," I said severely, "we're giving a dinner party tomorrow night."

"What's he serving?" Mr. Ambassador asked.

"Braised quail with crayfish. It's hard to make. And vegetable pâté to start with."

A funny look came over Mr. Ambassador.

'I'm really sorry," he said. "But to tell the truth, the dinner party slipped my mind. A minister is coming in tomorrow and he asked me to take him to Hamburger Hamlet. You'll have to manage without me."

"I suppose," I said, "you're going out afterwards to Swensons for a hot fudge sundae?"

"I believe that was mentioned in the telegram from Ottawa," he replied. "What can I do? Ambassadors are never masters in their own house."

"Unlike chefs," I said.

"Precisely."

You see Beverly, how chefs can cause more problems than one would think. Mr. Ambassador is showing up less and less at his own dinner parties. And people are beginning to talk. I think it's time for another face-off with Phillipe. He has to learn how to make spaghetti with big meat balls or else it's divorce.

I think if you sent us a bag of your bagels it might help our marriage.

Your best friend,
Sondra

Official and Non-official Dogs

Dear Beverly,

Don't ask me for an update on the private life of the pandas in the zoo because "wife of" is barred from entering. Ditto with Dumbarton Oaks and Swensen's ice cream store. I thought I had pull with the director of the National Portrait Gallery, but even he's thinking of putting cement trucks at the front of the place to keep me from coming in. It's not that I'm suspected of being a human bomb; it's just that "wife of" has become besotted over a creature living at the residence, Sweet Pea, the embassy dog, and I love to take him out on the leash.

Sweet Pea is not like any of the other dogs I've ever owned. He thinks of himself as belonging to government so his behavior is as cautious as a mid-management bureaucrat. His nature is certainly a contrast to Hector, the Airedale we owned in Ottawa.

Remember him, Beverly? Hector collected the flesh of joggers as trophies. Hector was more of a Clint Eastwood type—a real loner who would never allow anyone to take him for a walk on a leash. He preferred to lope eight miles to the shopping district and wait for the bad guys to come and make his day.

It was best to avoid him if I had an errand in the same district. I knew that Hector liked to keep to himself. Occasionally I'd join the outcry from cyclists, joggers and golden age groups carrying parcels, cursing the dog and his owners. But Hector had his code: whatever he did to anyone else, he never bit a member of the family. When he came home Hector gave us a glad but brief hello, because he had to go out again and clear the neighborhood of cats. Hector never sat at my feet, let alone jumped up beside me taking the only cushion on the sofa, like Sweet Pea, the embassy dog.

To tell you the truth, Beverly, I don't know if Sweet Pea knows what a cat or a jogger looks like. He's afraid to go outside alone even in his back yard. If the wind shifts slightly to the east, or a butterfly bumps into his nose, it's back to the silk cushion in the drawing room, near the air conditioning vent. I think a dog goes through a corruption of the soul living in an embassy. When it rains Sweet Pea's not ashamed to go for a walk wearing plastic baggies tied with elastics to his feet, as long as a human takes him out on the leash. The butler thought the baggies would protect the drawing room from being dirtied. Being an embassy dog, Sweet Pea understood. He knows it's important to look after government property. Mr. Ambassador wasn't so tolerant and said he would never walk a dog on Massachusetts Avenue wearing plastic baggies. It would give him, our country and the dog the ultimate wimp image.

I bought Sweet Pea from a lady in McLean, Va., who said he was a Tibetan Terrier. He might be a terrier to her and a terrier to me, but to real terriers like Hector, he's no terrier. Hector was all bite and no bark. Hector was never fool enough to give warning. On a quiet evening the only sound we ever heard was a jogger's scream, and then it was off to the emergency room again, trying to calm an hysterical male stranger with soothing words about Hector's recent rabies shots.

I realized that a Clint Eastwood-type dog wouldn't do in an embassy. When I bought Sweet Pea (even the name is a giveaway), I wanted to soothe myself. Mr. Ambassador had a fight the night before with his Prime Minister, and "wife of" thought he was going to be fired for sure. I needed a security blanket, and Sweet Pea is one of those hairy dogs who look the same from either end. I got him cheap because the lady told me he had an overbite problem. Since we still have no way of knowing whether he's coming or going, this is of no account.

As I mentioned, Beverly, there's something about living in an embassy that makes a dog go soft. For exercise, Hector used to follow the Greyhound buses on the highway; Sweet Pea follows the waiters carrying trays of canapés from the kitchen to the library. Embassy dogs are pompous and like the sound of their own bark. Popsie Tribble thought Sweet Pea needed a little more diplomatic training so she taught him not to bark at Powerful Job and Famous Names.

Now he threatens only decompressing former Mr. Secretaries, and the most junior members of Mr. Ambassador's political staff who are greeted with a high pitched hypocritical bark. It's disconcerting to have a dog so attuned to status, but what do you expect in Washington?

Hector, the Airedale Terrier, ate kibble from a bowl in the boiler room. Sweet Pea, the Tibetan Terrier, positions himself under a table in the dining room at a black-tie dinner waiting for a Powerful Job to hand him a rack of lamb.

I don't know whether you read about the event, Beverly, but there was a status dog show recently in Washington organized in honor of a charity. A Washington status dog show means that canine training, breeding and deportment don't count, so long as the dog's owned by someone powerful. Ambassadors are not really powerful in this city, but lip service to protocol is maintained, and even the dog show had a classification for embassy dogs. Of course, Ed Meese's dog got all the publicity, and I'm not even sure she's a thoroughbred. Anyway, I was all ready to take Sweet Pea to the dog show, but our foreign minister came into town that day and he took priority. Mr. Ambassador requisitioned a junior member of his staff to accompany the dog. Sweet Pea was annoyed and behaved badly. He used the junior staffer's leg as a fire hydrant and barked hysterically because he had to wait for Meese's dog to receive an award before the embassy dog contest got under way.

Sweet Pea still has a lot to learn. He may be an embassy dog but he's no diplomat.

Your best friend,
Sondra

The Lionel Portant Round-Tables

Dear Beverly,

Sorry to hear that the muffin craze is waning and George has no option but to retool the machinery in your mall basement stall into bagel-makers. Sonny Goldstone, who should know about these things, says that bagels have always had more market appeal than muffins. I'm sure you and George are doing the right thing, despite the capital investment.

I must say that, over the long haul, Sonny has been a steady friend, which is something I cannot say about Lionel Portant. I've already mentioned how many times he's walked away from me at parties, and then, when "wife of" maturely accepts the fact she's got something Portant is allergic to, he comes up and treats me like Princess Di. Portant's hot-and-cold technique is not only directed, I'm glad to say, at "wife of." Baron Spitte, who's never been too crazy about the Powerful Press, says that Lionel Portant has become too big for his boots. He's on the verge of being a media celebrity and shines on you only when he thinks you or your country are involved in some scandal. The last time Portant spoke to me was during our election, when one of the candidates was shown patting a lady's bum on the evening network news. You have to work hard for your country to get Portant's attention.

I'm not sure why Portant's pronouncements are treated with such respect. When I asked the Baron (I realize, Beverly, he's not an unbiased observer), the Baron said, "It's because he has a hooded personality. Which means people are never quite sure whether he's being prophetic or sanctimonious, profound or merely obscure, arrogant or self-confident, irresponsible or breaking a brilliant news story. Portant's genius is that he creates doubt in your own judgment."

Well, Beverly, not everyone thinks that Lionel has a hooded personality. Look at Popsie Tribble. She sent me a perplexing invitation, which reads: "Come to a Round-the-Table With Lionel Portant."

"What's that supposed to mean?" I asked when I saw her.

'I'm giving a series. You're lucky to be in on it. Every month I ask five Powerful Jobs, with "wives of" and a mixer couple — that's you and Mr. Ambassador — to listen to what Lionel Portant has to say. It's like having an Aspen Conference in Georgetown."

"Why should I go to lunch with Lionel when I can read and see him on the TV?"

"This is off-the-record stuff," Popsie announced.

"I thought White House Persons, Mr. Secretaries, Senators, even Mr. Ambassadors talk off-the-record, not the media."

"Lionel's just been to Cuba for four days," Popsie replied, "and was warned by Castro not to reveal all." Popsie sounded a little defensive.

"Have you become a Lionel Portant groupie?" I asked.

"He's been helpful to Dexter. And it's always good to give the Powerful Press a little boost."

Mr. Ambassador snorted when I told him about the Round Table. "Why doesn't Popsie ask Beverly, instead of Portant, to talk about Cuba? Didn't she go there for two weeks on one of those package holiday tours?"

Beverly, I've been living in Washington so long that I forgot we had diplomatic relations with Cuba. You must know more about Cuba than Portant. I remember you telling me that it was cheaper than the Mexican fat farm.

Anyway, we went to the Tribbles, albeit reluctantly, knowing that you'd make a better expert than Portant.

Beverly, you'll be happy to know that things didn't go as well as Popsie expected. Lionel flatly refused to say anything revealing about Cuba because of the contractual arrangements he's made with his publisher. He's saving all for the book. I'm not sure what the title will be, "Lionel Portant talks to Castro," or vice versa.

Melvin Thistle, Jr. from State got so angry with Portant that he called him a traitor.

Mrs. Portant, who's one of those protective "wives of" (I Stand By My Man, etc.) told Thistle Jr. to cover his weak chin by growing a Castro beard. Popsie didn't mind that because she likes a bit of controversy. But being the perfect hostess, she tried to make up for Portant's silence by making her own conversation livelier. The Cuba Libres loosened her tongue, and she begged a White House Person to let her sing *La Cucaracha* on Radio Marti.

Lionel Portant gave Dexter Tribble Cuban cigars as a present. I can tell you that he was pretty annoyed when Thistle Jr., after all the fuss, lifted half the box when he left.

Actually, Beverly, all was not for naught. Sonny Goldstone, who came to hear about the investment climate in Cuba, got so disgusted with the events that he became interested in your bagel venture. He offered to speak to the CEO at Nabisco about franchising you.

Your best friend,
Sondra

Vacation Mistakes

Dear Beverly,

As you know, a conversation with Popsie Tribble about even the most banal subject can destabilize "wife of." This time Popsie dropped in wearing her Issaye Miako jumpsuit (the new sloppy look, she explained) and asked what Mr. Ambassador and "wife of" were doing for our summer vacation.

"We're thinking of going to Europe in August," I said.

Popsie nearly choked on the lime in her Evian water. She never drinks the liquid that flows from Washington taps and claims that Perrier water is too gassy.

"Last year," she warned, "you had a nervous breakdown holidaying in the Hamptons. Now you're making another vacation mistake. The right people don't go to Europe in August, and only a fool would go this year."

"What do you mean?" I answered. "The airlines are already overbooked, and I've been scrambling to find a place to stay in Paris."

"My point exactly," Popsie said. "Europe will be over-run by all the wrong people. It's become too cheap."

Well, Beverly, that's why Mr. Ambassador wants to go, but I was afraid to say that to Popsie. I answered a little defensively, "Baron Spitte says Europe is not as cheap as you might think. They're jacking up the prices."

Popsie shook her head. "The only way an August vacation in Europe can be bearable is if you stay in one place and avoid the crowds. Visit Sonny Goldstone, who's leased a palazzo on the Brenta Canal, or one of those country homes in England — maybe Chatsfield, the Duke of Devonshire's place."

"Don't you have to be asked?"

"Certainly," Popsie said. "You just can't barge in."

I felt we had reached an impasse in our conversation so I asked her what she was doing.

"South Hampton," she said. "Unlike you, I feel perfectly at home there. And then we're going to Newport."

"Are you renting?" I asked, ignoring her aside.

"No, we're house guests. Much cheaper, except for the tips. Dexter says it's our year to economize."

I don't know why Popsie can get away with saying she wants a cheap vacation and "wife of" can't. But that's the way it is.

"Is anyone else making a vacation mistake besides us?" I asked.

"Joe Promisall," Popsie replied. "He's driving through Burgundy and Bordeaux visiting the wine cellars in the morning, taking in a one-star restaurant at noon and a two- or three-star in the evening."

"Why is that a vacation mistake?"

"Have you ever drunk Chambertin at 10 a.m., lunched on snails in garlic butter and pike quenelles in lobster sauce with a little Montrachet at lunch, driven through the heat in the afternoon and dined on tripe, preserved goose, 30 varieties of cheese and *Marquise au chocolat* in the evening? Eat it and die, I say."

"It sounds a bit rich," I agreed. "But haven't some of those restaurants changed to a lighter cuisine?"

"Nouvelle cuisine is even worse. Squashed red pepper mousse sitting in a muddy pool of mushroom purée. Why bother going to France at all? You can get the same mess right here on K Street."

"Is there anyone else making a vacation mistake?" I asked.

"Lionel Portant," Popsie said scornfully. "He thinks he's being chic doing this walking tour through Cornwall. It always rains and "wife of" Portant will have two inches of water in her evening bath, which will be tepid. She'll have to return to Rehoboth to get warm."

Beverly, I didn't tell Popsie about "wife of" Melvin Thistle, Jr., who probably has the best idea for a vacation. She's declared her bedroom in Cleveland Park a hotel room, put a Gideon bible in the night table, rented a TV with a huge screen, bought a little folding luggage rack and is paying her teen-ager to bring up room service. I understand she plans to stay there a month. Only one thing is holding her back. Melvin is having trouble finding some of those no-steal hangers.

You should take a lesson from "wife of" Thistle, Beverly, because I think George's sailboat is a vacation mistake. You're going to spend hours treading water while you scrub the sides of the boat with Brillo pads. I know that George likes to think he's the ruler of the wind and tide. But I remember when he sailed on the wrong side of a buoy and had to be hauled off a rock by the barge man.

Believe me, by the time you're finished your sailing vacation, the very phrase Tall Ships will make you throw up.

Your best friend,
Sondra